On the Threshold of
Adolescence

On the Threshold of
Adolescence

The Struggle for Independence
in the Twelfth Year

HERMANN KOEPKE

Translated by Catherine E. Creeger

ANTHROPOSOPHIC PRESS

This book is a translation of *Das zwölfte Lebensjahr:
Eintritt in die Pubertät* by Hermann Koepke. It was published
in German in 1989 by the Philosophisch-Anthroposophischer
Verlag at the Goetheanum in Dornach, Switzerland.
The translation is published with the author's permission.

Published in the United States by Anthroposophic Press

Library of Congress Cataloging-in-Publication Data

Koepke, Hermann.
    [Zwölfte Lebensjahr.   English]
    On the threshold of adolescence : the struggle for
independence in the twelfth year / Hermann Koepke :
translated by Catherine E. Creeger.
        Translation of: Das Zwölfte Lebensjahr.
    Includes index.
    ISBN 0-88010-357-4 (paper)
    1. Waldorf method of education. 2. Adolescence. 3. Sixth grade
(Education) 4. Classroom management. I. Title.
LB1029.W34K6513 1991
305.23'5–dc20   91-26276
                                                   CIP

CONTENTS

PART ONE

The Class

.

MOTTO

Typical symptoms: rebellious behavior toward adults (they're so unfair all of a sudden!); interest in the opposite sex—sometimes more, sometimes less; emotional ups and downs that are enough to drive you nuts—one minute you're flying high, the next you're down in the dumps; and feelings of inferiority.

You're slowly developing opinions of your own, and those grown-ups had better take them seriously. And then there's discrimination against teenagers. I know from experience how unpleasant and frustrating *that* is. For example, you can be hanging out with people your own age in the subway, and all of a sudden something or other makes you burst out laughing, and that's enough to make all hell break loose. Right and left, people start bitching and getting nasty. Or suppose you bump into some feisty old man by mistake—he lets off a string of obscenities like you wouldn't think people that age would even *know* and gives you a real hard poke in the ribs. And people in stores don't want to wait on you, and they're unfriendly about it when they finally do. Things like that never happen to little kids. . . .

(from a fourteen-year-old's notebook)

PREFACE

In my twenty years as a class teacher in Waldorf schools, I had many opportunities for exchanging ideas with parents, students, artists, and doctors, and learned how eager they all were for a real-life glimpse into what goes on in a Rudolf Steiner school. I hope this book will answer some of their questions. While I was working on it, it developed into the story of Suzanne Kulp (a class teacher whose students are just turning twelve) and Harriet (an older teacher who is Suzanne's mentor.) Further scenes developed: Sitting in on Suzanne's main lesson, a teachers' meeting, a parents' meeting, and two home visits.

Although all the characters in the story are fictional, the scenario is based on reality. Each single incident in the book is based on real-life events and actual experiences.

Hermann Koepke
Dornach, Michaelmas 1989

| *1* |

An Excellent Teacher Runs into Trouble

No one on the faculty doubted that Suzanne was an excellent teacher. Anyone going by in the hallway or on the stairs could hear how wonderfully her class could recite, as if they were all speaking with one voice. Her blackboard drawings were imaginative, and her storytelling kept the children spellbound—surely signs of a quality education in progress. In addition, although the class had reached the age when the piles of notebooks, essays, math assignments, and dictations waiting for correction could assume monumental proportions, Suzanne was unusually conscientious about getting around to it all and perhaps even a bit pedantic—she even made a point of correcting the students' corrections! Of course, she was well prepared when she entered the classroom each morning. Discipline was strict; she had the class in hand. It seemed beside the point to ask whether she was getting through to her students as individuals.

As a rule, a class in a Rudolf Steiner school is taught by the same teacher from grades 1 through 8, with more and more extra subject teachers contributing as the children progress through the grades. When Suzanne took the class a bit more than five years ago, in her first year as a teacher, this group of children had been first graders. But now the children were changing so much and so fast, all of a sudden. Some of the girls were almost as tall as she was.

So far, Suzanne had never been through any kind of a crisis with the class except in the third grade, when the children were nine-going-on-ten. Back then, she had gotten the impression that some of them could have been doing much better if they had only been making more of an effort; by now, however, most of them were keeping up with the class again. After that year, the class had grown together in a new way and developed into a much stronger group than it had been before the crisis. And now, as long as Suzanne did not insist that girls sit next to boys or vice versa, things almost always went smoothly in class. The youngsters continued to accept her authority as a matter of course since Suzanne was so considerate of them and such a cheerful soul. The children knew that their well-being meant everything to her, and there had been no indication that their parents had any concerns or grounds for complaint.

But recently Suzanne had started to feel vaguely uneasy inside, and there were times when teaching took a lot more out of her than it used to. She began to wonder whether it was simply an occupational hazard of teaching this age group, or if there was something she wasn't really approaching the right way. At first her doubts were very faint, not something constantly eating away at her self-confidence; however, as time went on, they became more and more frequent and left her totally exhausted, as if all the strength had been drained out of her.

As always, Suzanne talked her troubles over with her friend Kathy, who shared an apartment with her. They had been friends ever since they were in college together, and now they both taught at the same school. Talking with Kathy always cheered Suzanne up; for a while, teaching was easy again, and her vague uneasiness seemed like a mere figment of the imagination.

It hadn't occurred to Suzanne to have this kind of conversation with someone older and more experienced. Perhaps that would have been much less easy and natural, but it might have made Suzanne aware that her uneasiness was a sign that her students were on the brink of a new developmental phase. There was definitely something going on, something that confronts every class teacher when the group reaches the preadolescent stage. However, Suzanne, a first-time teacher, was taking it too personally to be able to come to grips with it effectively. "Puberty" was synonymous with "problems" as far as she was concerned, and she had given no more specific thought to where the problems were actually coming from. "I'm just going to have to deal with it, no matter what you want to call it," she thought. "I can't just say,'Oh, it's only puberty' and forget about it; that would be a cop-out." On the other hand, she may also have overlooked the very first warning signs of puberty because she simply had not counted on them showing up in this particular way.

But together with her difficulties in class, the events that followed really did give her cause to reflect. "Somehow, the parents don't trust me the way they used to," she thought. "They're being really abrupt with me and almost reproachful all of a sudden."

One afternoon Kathy reported that several people had been trying to reach Suzanne. One of them was the mother of a boy in her class, and she had sounded pretty upset. Suzanne went straight to the phone and dialed the number. Scott's mother answered immediately and proceeded to take Suzanne to task for telling one of Scott's classmates to cut Scott's hair. Suzanne was practically speechless—she hadn't told anyone to do anything of the sort although she had caught a glimpse of some suspicious goings-on with scissors when she had stopped in on their arts and crafts class. She reproached herself for not having intervened. Still, she felt as if she had been hit by a bolt of lightning out of a clear blue sky.

Scott had come home very distressed and close to tears, his mother reported. As his class teacher, Suzanne must be aware that her son was having a hard time in class, and she sincerely hoped there would be no further incidents. Things didn't seem to be going too well with the class, anyway. Suzanne explained the situation as best she could and tried to get Scott's mother to calm down. But the episode struck a discordant note with her, and she couldn't get it out of her mind.

Several days later, she got a note from a usually friendly and helpful mother asking why her daughter was always the one "selected" to stay behind and sweep the classroom. Alice was always coming home late because she missed the bus. Suzanne was totally taken aback. Again, that was not quite the way it had been. Only once, and for very good reasons, had she asked that girl to stay behind and clean up.

Both mothers had taken their childrens' word as gospel without asking her if that was all there was to it. "Why don't they ask me about my side of the story?" wondered Suzanne. "They have never simply accused me like this before."

These two incidents were just the beginning of a series of unpleasantries. The gym teacher complained about the lack of discipline in the class. Whenever he had something to explain, only part of the group listened; the rest were messing around in the gym and using the equipment without supervision. He had forbidden this in no uncertain terms because it could be very dangerous. Also, the number of unexcused absences among the girls was conspicuous. What, he demanded of Suzanne, were they up to during the time when they were supposed to be in gym class?

Next, a father came to see her and complained about how little his daughter was learning in the sixth grade and how flighty and unresponsive she had become. When he had asked her how many pounds there were in a ton, she'd simply shrugged. Other concerned parents had noticed similar deficits in other subjects: spelling, grammar, French. . . .

It would be an exaggeration to say that Suzanne's confidence was totally eroded and that from then on she was nervous every time she set foot in the classroom. That was not the case, and yet it was clear from looking at her that something was wrong, and she was showered with well-meaning sympathy and advice. "You don't look very well at all, you know. I noticed it the last time I saw you. Make sure you see a good doctor, all right?"

Meanwhile, Suzanne was trying to be extra conscientious in how she prepared her presentations. She broke the three-step word problems she was introducing in arithmetic down into the smallest possible steps and discussed them one at a time, but all her careful explanations were as good as useless. The students whose interest she was trying hardest to catch were the ones who paid the least attention. As they became less and less receptive, Suzanne's voice got shriller and shriller in spite of herself. Some of the girls said straight out that they could not understand problems like that and refused to try. One girl, who enjoyed a special standing among her peers because her physical development had started early, seemed to be the one spearheading the resistance. Giggling broke out behind Suzanne's back. She felt more and more uncertain and was getting less and less able to get through to some of the youngsters. Uncertainty widened the gap between her and the students. Her inability to bridge it turned her uncertainty into fear, and the vicious cycle was complete. She was totally exhausted by the end of the day.

Fortunately, Kathy was there to hear her out and share her despair. "I really can't go on; I'm at the end of my rope!" Nothing Kathy could say seemed to do any good, so instead of comforting Suzanne, she tried to cheer her up. "I've got a good idea—you can brush up on how to teach three-step word problems and become our remedial math teacher!" The effect of that suggestion was like a cold shower, and Suzanne was cured on the spot. "Any other bright ideas?" she laughed. Her friend was laughing too. "Not for today, Sue. But you know, whenever I get into a situation like that, I take as my motto, 'Never mind—things could get worse, and they probably will!'"

* * *

Suzanne knew that she could handle herself well in all kinds of conversations. Young and appealing as she was, she had never yet found herself in a situation she couldn't handle. She was able—much to her advantage—to listen silently to much that would have aroused someone else to indignation and then make a snappy comeback. But she was too clever to delude herself, so she slowly began to consider the factors involved, trying to figure out why she had found herself almost utterly at a loss. From the bottom of her heart she hoped that this would all blow over and that teaching would become a fulfilling experience once again.

That was not how things were to be, however. The girls who had skipped gym class had been caught shoplifting, and when Suzanne investigated the incident in class, she found that still more children had been involved. She felt chills run up and down her spine.

She made the children who had confessed to shoplifting stay in at recess. "Is this the first time you've gone shoplifting?" Some nodded, some shook their heads. None of them spoke. "What did you do with the things you took?" A few children laid things on the desk—erasers, pencils, still without saying a word. "Is that all?" A few more items appeared. "What do you have to say for yourselves?" The youngsters looked at each other; a few ventured hesitant comments. Suzanne was suddenly overcome with the feeling she'd been having ever since the fiasco with the word problems, and she raised her voice. "There are legal penalties for shoplifting, you know. I want to know why you did it!" A couple of questions in that tone of voice were enough to make them all clam up totally. Meanwhile, the short recess was over and the rest of the class was trickling in. "You're all going to stay after school tomorrow," Suzanne snapped. "This investigation is not over yet." The whole class was restless, and finally one boy spoke up, saying it was unfair that only the ones who had confessed to stealing would have to stay after school the next day, while the ones who were just as guilty but hadn't admitted it got to go home.

Suzanne went over these conversations in her mind again as she was getting ready for school the next day. It was clear, she realized, that being strict and putting pressure on the children had exactly the opposite effect from what she had intended. She had wanted everything to come to light, but instead the girls and boys had become totally inaccessible. Now that she was able to take a step back from the situation, she knew that her reaction had been unfortunate, and she hoped it wasn't already too late to switch from reacting to positive action.

Just before the end of school that day, she spoke to the whole class again. "It's going to be impossible for us to have any real class spirit unless we know the whole truth about the shoplifting. That means that everyone who was involved needs to stay after class so we can go on talking about it. Some of you have already admitted you did it—you had the guts to confess to having taken things, and that goes a long way toward making amends for the damage. If we work together, we'll be able to make it up to the department store. But we're dependent on those of you who also stole but haven't been able to say so yet. I want to ask you to be strong enough to admit it, too. I don't want to get into any big investigations and I don't want you to start accusing each other. I'm trusting each one of you to find the courage to tell the truth."

A muted discussion ensued as to who had or had not been involved. Suzanne let the boys and girls talk among themselves for a while and then opened the door. Finally only the perpetrators remained; their classmates had all left. There were a few more of them than there had been the day before, and among them were three students

Suzanne had always thought could have been doing better if they would just make more of an effort. It had been like that ever since third grade. Suzanne wondered again why she had never really been able to get through to these three.

This time the youngsters were ready to tell her all about their excursions to the department store. They put the rest of the stolen items on her desk or promised to bring them in the next day. Again she asked why they had done it, and they shrugged. "Just because." "Don't know." "I just went along with the rest." One boy said he had thought it would be exciting to see if they'd get caught. Suzanne spent some time showing them how unworthy and ill-considered their motives had been. The next day she and the youngsters returned all the items to the store manager.

That was the end of the incident, but it had been the last straw for Suzanne. She decided to present all her difficulties with the class to the group of teachers responsible for running the school.

| 2 |

In the Faculty Meeting

Suzanne sat at the big round table with her colleagues, most of whom were older than she. Her courage faltered as she brought her lengthy and detailed report to a close, and she thought to herself, "I just can't do everything that's being asked of me. I'm really losing my grip." She glanced up and looked around at the solemn faces of her fellow teachers. They had heard her out without commenting, and now, as if of one accord, they all sat looking down at the table as they considered what she had said. There was a long silence before one of the older teachers spoke up.

"You know, I've been hearing this same thing for quite a few years now, and although different people put it a bit differently, the gist of it is always the same. With the onset of puberty, something happens that very quickly creates a rift between teacher and students, parents and child, home and school, or even between the parents themselves or between subject teachers and the class teacher. This tendency toward divisiveness is everywhere." He paused for a moment before continuing. "It's unfortunate when the adults responsible for educating young people are not in agreement among themselves, as is so often the case. You might even say that as a general rule, the children's crisis of puberty ends up being secondary to the crisis the grown-ups have to work out among themselves, which complicates the issue and only adds to the difficulties. You wouldn't believe how often I've watched parents start to fall into two opposing camps when their children reach sixth grade.

"At puberty, young people are confronted with the task of educating themselves for the first time in their lives. It's an extremely significant stage in a person's biography when self-education begins. But where are these young people supposed to get their sense of direction from if the adults around them can't agree, or if one significant adult is inconsistent? Of course, teachers and parents may not be quite up to the job and have to keep on learning themselves—a certain amount of critical self-examination is absolutely in order. But there is only one way to build up mutual trust, and that is for us and the parents, the community of educators surrounding these youngsters, to spend some time together thinking about what happens as children grow up. That's how we can get out of being stuck in ourselves and start to develop the right kind of dedication to the young people. Together we need to become an organ similar to an eye, which is able to perceive other things only to the extent that it does not perceive itself." He looked around the table and spoke with certainty and deliberation. "We have to do something differently in our school. I'd like to suggest that at the beginning of the fifth grade, we get a head start on educating both the class teacher and the parents about puberty, which is just approaching for their youngsters. We would need to have a special parents' meeting for that purpose. And we would need to make sure that the younger teachers who are going through this difficult and dangerous phase with a class for the first time are accompanied by older, more experienced faculty members who can be their friends and advisors, visit their classes, and discuss with them all the details of what needs to be done differently to make their teaching approach appropriate to that age group. If we don't, I'm afraid we may soon find ourselves with no teachers left. It's not that you've done anything wrong, Suzanne," he said, turning to her. "This is a sin of omission on the part of the whole faculty."

Another lengthy silence ensued. Then, at first somewhat hesitantly, others began to speak, offering their assessment of specific situations: "Having the class speak in unison was all well and good in the lower grades. But now you can't really go on in the same way without running the risk of those newly awakening young individualities being drowned out in the torrent of common recitation. Then they'll react by expressing themselves as individuals in whatever ways remain open to them, and this will lead to all kinds of discipline problems.

"Don't take it wrong, Suzanne—we're glad you're using speech in the classroom, but you need to take the age of the class into consideration and introduce different techniques more in keeping with your students' phase of development. For instance, now would be the time to find a way to introduce dialogues, paving the way for dramatic speaking. The main thing in drama is that the characters have to assert themselves against each other, so two opposing groups could take turns speaking, or two students could be asked to conduct a simple dialogue, like the Greek speakers in the agora. That would be one way of getting youngsters involved who like to draw attention to themselves and might otherwise be causing a distraction. Meanwhile, the rest of the class could take the role of the audience, agreeing or disagreeing with the speakers. Ideally, you should all work these scenes out in class together."

"But at this critical age when everything starts to fall apart, you sometimes simply have to take things as they are," interjected Harriet, a retired teacher. "The more you get into explaining your explanations, the way you did with those three-step problems, the more likely you are to turn your students off. After all, a lot of them, especially the girls, aren't at all interested in the logical steps you have to go through. They have, umm, quite different things on their minds, shall we say." She paused for effect, and smiled as she continued, "As a rule, girls stay with pictorial thinking longer than boys do. So turn the problem into a picture that will catch their attention! Draw it right on the board.

Line 1: Three of those lipsticks with the purple cases cost nine dollars.

Line 2: One lipstick costs?

Line 3: Thirteen lipsticks cost? I chose the number thirteen on purpose so that there would be enough to go around. There are sixteen girls in your class, aren't there? And three of your young ladies are wearing lipstick already. You have to do it with humor. If you can catch their interest that way, it will get them going in arithmetic."

"But I don't want to encourage the other girls to use lipstick, do I?" Suzanne objected.

"Don't worry; you can afford to rely much more on humor and much less on what you think you ought to be doing. The point is to get the girls' attention, and you have to catch them where their thoughts are at the moment, don't you see?"

Suzanne still wasn't sure. "But what if they all start coming to school all painted up? What will the other teachers say? Not to mention their parents!"

"Just make sure you time it right for Halloween," commented Harriet drily. General merriment drowned her out for a moment. "But I don't think that will happen. After all, the girls are going to feel as if you've seen through their tricks if you pull it off naturally enough. And the amount of money involved will certainly make an impression on them. After all, it comes to thirty-nine dollars; that's not peanuts! And if worst comes to worst, all you have to do is use bright red lipstick yourself for a while, and make sure you wear a sweater that goes with it—bright green, or something like that! You'll see that wearing lipstick will lose its appeal for them pretty quickly. After all, you've been cultivating their sense of what's beautiful for years; now you'll find it coming back to you in the form of their own judgments. I bet at least a couple of your students would come up to you and say, 'Miss Kulp, you look absolutely terrible! You can't come to school again tomorrow looking like that!'"

"So we must leave the children free to develop opinions of their own about what's right and what's wrong, even if they're tempted to go out and do something dumb?" Suzanne asked dubiously.

"That's exactly what I mean. You're right to be concerned that they won't always assess the situation correctly—of course they won't, but that's not the point. The point is to give them the space to express their personal feelings and exercise their own judgment, even if it's a bit off track. A little humor on your part will always straighten things out. From now on, their own judgment should be allowed to take center stage more and more often. Your own authority used to be what set all the standards, but now you have to start withdrawing it slowly. You'll notice I said slowly—being able to come to independent conclusions and to be fully self-directed isn't something that happens overnight."

One of the foreign language teachers concurred heartily: "I teach in all the different grades, and I notice how important the teacher's authority is in the lower classes. But when the youngsters enter puberty, that all changes. Of course they still need a certain amount of guidance, but they also want to experience a different kind of authority. Humor allows a teacher to get down off her saint's pedestal and join her students on their own level. You become their partner, to a certain extent, but by kindling their enthusiasm with your sense of humor you gain a new and different kind of authority. You used to be the one who decided what was beautiful and what was ugly, and that was all there was to it. Now the children want to make these decisions on their own. They want to express their own opinions about what they like and what they don't like."

Suzanne was thinking hard. Relying on humor instead of authority—how was that supposed to work with this age group? She was about to say something, but Harriet spoke up first. "Teachers can use humor like salt," she said with a nod to the language teacher, "but nobody thinks it's funny if you dump too much salt in the soup. There's also something else that can help a teacher who has lost credibility with the class.

"Just think of the subjects we use for storytelling in the Waldorf schools—fairy tales in the first grade, legends and fables in the second, the story of creation in the third, Norse mythology in the fourth, and Greek mythology in the fifth. But when we get to where your class is now, the stories take a totally different direction. I'm overstating the case a bit, but as soon as you study the Trojan War near the end of grade 5, the gods and all the other supersensible beings suddenly retreat behind the scenes. In the earlier grades you talked about all the supersensible beings that influence our lives, guiding and even determining what we do. You talked about angels and saints and the Savior, and about God the Father and the Norse and Greek gods. But now suddenly something different happens.

"You all know the story: The Greeks besieged Troy for ten years without either side being able to defeat the other. Then Odysseus suggested using cunning instead of strength to prevail against the enemy—cunning instead of pitched battle. I'm sure you experienced a variety of reactions from your students; some were for it and some against. But the Trojan horse was built, and the Trojans failed to see through the deception and took the horse for a sacrificial offering to Athena. This is where causality begins to play a role in the story, and it's just this ability to think in terms of cause and effect that your students are waking up to. That's what makes them able to ask whether this deception was right or wrong, whether it was justified or not.

"When the Trojans were pulling the horse in through the city gates, its wheels got stuck on the threshold. With every tug they gave, it stuck again, and a metallic clink came from the wooden horse. But the Trojans suspected nothing and pulled the horse right into the middle of their city. So, what were the Trojans thinking—and what were they incapable of thinking? What about the Greeks? Were they different? Those are the kinds of questions you could ask the children.

"As the story continues, we get an example of the exact opposite of causative thinking. The horse stops in front of the king's palace, and Cassandra the prophetess comes storming out. She is a tragic figure indeed—she has the ability to see into the future but lacks the strength to change anything, to intervene in real life. In confused images, she speaks of a river of blood pouring out of the horse and engulfing the city. I think you can see what I'm getting at—an old pictorial state of consciousness confronts self-conscious human thinking, which is just beginning to wake up. The visionary consciousness of Cassandra, which sees both destiny and the divine in external events, has had its day, and therefore Troy is defeated. Thinking, which is initially all mixed up with lies and deception, begins to light up in individual human beings. This story documents the odyssey of thinking on its journey of purification until the 'god within,' Socrates' daimon, can speak in all purity."

Suzanne was impressed. She began to realize why the class had become more and more critical of her depictions of divine beings and in fact had begun to reject them outright. Even her imaginative blackboard drawings of the Greek gods, which had captured their attention to begin with, had no longer interested more than a couple of the girls at most. The boys had obviously turned their attention to other aspects of the lesson and had come to school with big books full of architectural photographs. They had drawn the columns and capitals of the temples and had wanted to know exactly what the Greek statues had looked like. It was obvious that they had been looking for something quite different from what Suzanne had been offering them. The whole class had been impressed with Socrates and his teachings, however, and when Suzanne copied a drawing of his distinctive head on the board, everyone had been attentive and appreciative.

"'I have enjoyed the advantages of the laws of Athens for a whole lifetime; why should I disdain them now that they are being applied to my disadvantage?'" Harriet was quoting Socrates. "That was his view of the law, and that was why he passed up a well thought-out opportunity to escape and instead drank the cup of hemlock. Even today, after more than two thousand years have gone by, his attitude makes a very deep impression.

Now that you're teaching sixth grade, make sure you don't overlook the story of young Manlius. General Manlius had laid down the law that engaging the enemy in single combat was punishable by death. Then his own son killed an opponent in a duel, and his father the general chose to abide by his own law and condemned his son to death. Not only that, but his son, who had restored the honor of Rome in that duel, was in agreement with the verdict. 'I have won the wreath and deserve my death,' as Conrad Ferdinand Meyer wrote in his ballad 'Manlius Rides to His Death.' The attitude of this father and his son is really extraordinary—they both submitted to the authority of the law.

"The sacred agreements we make and must abide by at all costs are a different aspect of authoritative guidance. Keeping these agreements rests on the fact that teachers and students are equal in the eyes of the law. Both teachers and students are expected to get to school on time. Students must hand in their assignments on time and teachers must correct them promptly; the teacher must live up to her end of the bargain as an example to the students.

The basic equality in these agreements gives the teacher the right to insist that they be carried out consistently.

"So you see, a lot of different factors play into a teacher's legitimate authority. Consistency is the last thing I mentioned, and consistency is based on the rationale behind something. However, a rationale is worthless unless it is readily understandable, and children are only capable of understanding reasoning after their ability to think in terms of cause and effect has developed. Giving reasons for everything would have been a mistake in the earlier grades, but it becomes a must at this point. But we don't want to set up a rigid system; that's why humor is so important. It's all right if the old authority comes down off her pedestal, because we have every reason to hope that the new authority will take over soon."

"There's something missing in the story you told as an example, though," said one of the class teachers. "There's no mercy or leniency in it. If we as a faculty were to act like your General Manlius, the shoplifters or at least the ringleaders would have to be expelled from school, and that wouldn't be right at all. Of course we'll have to have a very serious word with these youngsters, but it's also up to us to provide moral guidance and support."

The handwork teacher had something to add: "Once when I had to give some students a good talking-to, I made the mistake of saying something like, 'You're really terrible people; just get out of my sight,' and I was never really able to cope with those kids after that. We can't do that; we can't condemn them for doing what they did, we can only condemn their actions. We have to make that absolutely clear to them and help them understand what they did. But there's another step we have to take after that. We have to work with them to figure out what to do to rectify the situation, and it's important to show them that they'll be able to feel good about themselves again afterward, so that the goodness inside won't continue to be compromised by this one misstep."

"That's what I think, too," said Harriet. "The youngsters must understand that while we can't condone their actions, we're not condemning them as people, as individuals. And I also agree that we have an obligation to provide whatever moral support they need in this situation. Depending on how things are at home, that's not necessarily so easy for parents to do. But let's go back to the subject of leniency for a minute. I can still recall an old fellow teacher of mine saying in his inimitable way, 'When teachers are too lenient, you can see all their little inconsistencies and wishiwashinesses sticking up on top of their heads like toadstools.' It's difficult but very important for us to be consistent and forgiving at the same time. In the Oberufer Paradise play God the Father punishes Adam and Eve for their transgression by having them driven out of Paradise in spite of the fact that He created them and had the greatest possible love for them. If He hadn't acted with such rigorous consistency, human beings would have failed to develop some very important qualities." She looked around the table with a searching gaze. "The angel Gabriel shows no sign of mercy until the very end of the play, when he says, 'I shall recall you late and slow.'"

The older teacher who had opened the conversation spoke up again. "I would like to ask our friend Harriet, who spoke so eloquently on the subject of old and new authority, to be Suzanne's mentor for a while. Otherwise we're in danger of doing too much theorizing about this important transitional phase when what Suzanne needs are some concrete suggestions on how to adapt her main lesson. And we also need to think about the difficulties the special-subject teachers have been having with this class. Suzanne may need to hold the reins quite differently now than before, and that applies to the other teachers as well. If Suzanne has been holding the reins too tightly, it may not be easy to make the transition."

The faculty agreed that Harriet should visit Suzanne's class and make suggestions, and that she would also help Suzanne prepare a special meeting for the parents of the class to discuss the shoplifting incident as well as what to expect more generally from youngsters on the brink of puberty. Home visits, it was suggested, would be particularly important right now.

The school physician summarized what they had been talking about. "It's normal to have difficulties during puberty," she said. "It's actually much worse for children who seem to sail through this developmental phase without noticing it, for whom everything stays more or less the same. That's true not only of adolescence, but also of the crisis that can occur around age nine. If these transitions don't take place, the children are in for much more serious problems later on, problems that can be much more difficult to deal with than what we're facing now. These transitional phases are a bit like being born—pain is a natural and necessary part of the process. That's why it's important for children to learn that renunciation can be meaningful, rather than having all of life's little difficulties removed for them. For example, children who have been permitted to go through the usual childhood illnesses tend to do much better than the ones who've been vaccinated against everything. We really need to do some thinking about what 'separation' and 'becoming independent' mean, and how they happen.

"But let me tell you something funny instead of just theorizing. Someone mentioned the Paradise play a little while ago, and you all know that I played the devil every year for a number of years. Before one performance, I dreamed that I was onstage and that Eve refused to accept the apple I broke off and offered to her. I did everything I could to make her take it in her hand, but she simply would not. I held it up to her mouth and she wouldn't bite. It just didn't work; she refused to be tempted! In the end, I walked out into the audience crying, 'What am I supposed to do now? Human evolution cannot continue!'"

Suzanne felt much better after this meeting with her colleagues. Knowing that it wasn't just her, that what she had been taking so personally was actually an inherently difficult situation for others as well, made her feel much more able to face her class again.

SUGGESTED READING:

Christmas Plays from Oberufer, tr. A.C. Harwood, Rudolf Steiner Press, 1973.

Norbert Glas, Conception, Birth and Early Childhood, Anthroposophic Press, 1985.

Werner Glas, The Waldorf School Approach to History. Anthroposophic Press, 1980.

Michaela Glöckler and Wolfgang Goebel, A Guide to Child Health, Anthroposophic Press, 1990.

Joan Salter, The Incarnating Child, Hawthorne Press, 1989.

Rudolf Steiner, The Child's Changing Consciousness and Waldorf Education, Anthroposophic Press, 1988.

Wilhelm zur Linden, When a Child Is Born, Harper, 1989.

| 3 |

Harriet's Visit to Suzanne's Class

Harriet was sitting in the back row. Suzanne, standing up front, was much more nervous about her visit than the students were. The class was going to have to get a real talking-to before their main lesson. The school had received a notice from the police; neighbors of the school had been complaining that some students had not been obeying traffic regulations. Additional traffic police were being assigned to the area.

Suzanne had spent the previous evening turning the problem over and over in her mind. Should she present it humorously, or in terms of cause and effect, or as a matter of "sacred agreement"? Or should she simply read the letter from the police? Now she had to decide on one of the four options. The class was waiting in suspense, surprised that she hadn't started the main lesson.

"First of all, I'd like to welcome our visitor, who will be spending a couple of days with us. I'm very glad to have her here. Unfortunately, though, I also have to announce a visitor we may not be so happy to see." ("Uh oh, is the eurythmy teacher coming too?" whispered a smart aleck. His neighbors giggled.)

"I don't think you have to worry about the eurythmy teacher, but you might be a little bit afraid of the police."

"The police?" (Wide-eyed innocence.)

"Yes, the police have announced their intention to visit this class. They've found out that some of you have great hidden talents. Apparently there are some gifted acrobats in this class who specialize in bicycle stunts, and the police would like to have a word with them." She had caught the children's attention. "One of the stunts they'd like to see is called 'riding the rack.' It's especially impressive when great big Bob is little Lisa's passenger." (Laughter.) "Or when Heather and Lauren ride no hands and really close together so they almost bump into each other, but their handlebars don't even touch. And I almost forgot the special attraction—riding in formation. That's when three of you—or was it four?—ride along next to each other without a care in the world, even if the cars behind you are beeping and honking because they don't dare to pass you. I wish I had the nerves you guys have. Yours must be made of steel." (Smirks.) "Anyway, that's what the police are interested in." (Comment: "Well, it's about time!") "And our school is attracting a lot of attention because some of our students make such rude remarks when pedestrians dare to say anything to them." Now the class was silent.

After a pause, Suzanne continued in a quiet but determined voice. "Joking aside, you all know what I'm talking about. You can't just ride your bikes wherever you want whenever you want; there are rules and regulations for riding in traffic just as there are rules to a game. You have a right to complain when someone breaks the rules in sports but, on the other hand, you're expected to obey the rules yourselves, too. Anybody who ignores the rules is being unfair.

"Here's the letter the police sent to our school:'In view of the above-mentioned circumstances we urge you to make every effort to encourage your students to abide by traffic regulations. In future, additional traffic officers will be assigned to your area, and all violations will be reported to the office of the public prosecutor for youthful offenders.'" Suzanne put the letter back in its envelope. "May I suggest that you reserve your creative activity for the classroom or the stage and let fair play be the rule when you're on the streets?"

The class was silent for a moment. Then she asked them to stand up for morning verse. They got up quietly and looked around at each other with a bit of trepidation before speaking the verse with the two teachers.

After having the class practice a song in several parts, Suzanne did some speech exercises that she had selected to show the contrast between biting sharpness and rounded, knowing self-restraint. For the former, she had chosen "Split and bite and cut and stab with sharp and blinding spears;" for the latter, "Round the far and vast horizon showers sound." First she asked the boys to speak with cutting sharpness and the girls to respond with all-knowing superiority, and then she reversed the roles. "Knowing" was supposed to be spoken in such a way that it overcame the "sharpness" of what had just been spoken—not an easy thing to do. After these preliminary exercises, the whole class recited Rudolf Steiner's parable about the origin of evil:

The Origin of Evil

Once upon a time there lived a man
who pondered much about the world.
His brain was tortured most of all
by his desire to know the origin of evil;
But he could give himself on this no answer.
"The whole world comes from God," so argued he,
"and God can only have the good within Himself.
Then how do evil men come from the good?"
Time and again he pondered, all in vain.
The answer could not be discovered.
One day it came to pass, this gloomy thinker
upon his way beheld a tree,
which was in conversation with an axe.
And mark! the axe was saying to the tree:
"What is impossible for you to do, that I can do.
I can fell you, but not you me."
The tree then gave this answer to the haughty axe:
"A year ago a man cut out the wood
from which he made your handle
out of my body, with another axe."
And when the man had heard this speech
a thought arose within his soul
he could not clearly put in words.
It gave, however, answer to his question
How evil can derive from good.

Suzanne divided the tree's conversation with the axe
between boys and girls, first one way and then the other.
She could hear how the youngsters enjoyed pitting their
strength against each other as they spoke.

After that, the class got out their big main-lesson

notebooks and showed her their assignment, a polygon inscribed in a circle divided into twenty-four parts. Teachers and students walked around the room looking at what everyone had done. Suzanne was surprised at how interested the children were in each other's work. To conclude that part of the lesson, she showed the class the notebooks of several students who had put a lot of effort into the assignment, but also a few belonging to youngsters from whom she had expected something better. At that point, Harriet jotted something down in her notebook for the first time that morning.

"What do we have to do to make sure a line comes out straight?" Suzanne asked the class. "You have to turn the pencil a bit while you're drawing," a lot of the youngsters answered. "That's right, but what if it still comes out crooked?" Suzanne put her ruler down in the middle of a page, and turned the pencil as she drew the line. She showed it to the class. It was definitely not straight. "How come?" Eventually the youngsters discovered that an underlying page was wrinkled and had distorted the line as it was being drawn. "Good for you!" said Suzanne. "You're really on the ball this morning." She positioned the ruler again, making sure that all the pages in the notebook were perfectly smooth, turned the pencil as she drew the line—and it still came out crooked. This time the children were not so quick to figure out what she'd done wrong. It took a couple of demonstrations and some lively discussion before they figured out that she had changed the angle of the pencil to the page very sharply as she was drawing, so that its point had not always been right up against the ruler. "For tomorrow, I want you to see if you can discover some other things that will make it come out wrong."

She had also asked the class to bring in flat pieces of wood that they had sanded to a smooth finish, and they were all wondering what they were going to do with them. Instead of getting into all kinds of explanations, Suzanne simply held up what she had done for them to look at. She had pounded tacks into her board at regular intervals along the sides of an equilateral triangle and had strung colored thread between the tacks on one side and those on another according to a certain pattern. She asked the class to figure out the pattern for themselves. Most of the boys did their thinking out loud, but most of the girls were silent. Then they all got to take tacks and hammers, and soon the room was full of the sound of tacks being driven into the wood.

It was soon obvious that the girls were generally more skillful than the boys; in fact, one boy who was extremely bright suddenly seemed to have two left hands. Some of the youngsters were already finished before the bell rang for recess. Suzanne asked the others to finish the project for homework. Very briefly, she showed them another pattern she had made and said that they would work on that one tomorrow. "Oh jeez, how exciting," said the boy who had been all thumbs.

Suddenly there was a crash, and one of the girls went sprawling on the floor. Her chair had come apart. Suzanne made sure she wasn't hurt, put the broken chair to one side without commenting, and asked the class to put their things away. It took some time until they were all standing behind their chairs and ready to close the lesson with a verse they recited together.

As the kids streamed out of the classroom, Harriet came up to Suzanne's desk. "You've already put into practice a lot of what we talked about last time," she said approvingly. "As soon as you have time, I'd like to talk with you about today's lesson." "Can we do that after recess in the teachers' room? Right now I have recess duty." "I'll come with you," said Harriet, "It's amazing how well you can get to know the children at recess." They got their coats and went outside, where they stood with their backs to the building and looked around the playground.

The first graders were still clustered around their teacher; the second graders had let go of the apron strings and were playing catch. Some of the fourth and fifth graders were running relays, their movements graceful and harmonious. There was a distinct difference in the movement patterns of the youngsters after the fifth grade. Some of the sixth graders had suddenly shot up and were long-legged and lanky; they seemed to tip forward slightly from the waist up as they ran, and sometimes they stumbled. Even when they were just strolling across the playground, you could notice a subtle groping for balance at each step. They had lost the grace of the younger children, and seemed to go abruptly from standing still to tearing around like mad, with no transition whatsoever. The next older grades followed the same patterns of movement, and it was only in the upper grades of the high school that the occasional movements of the young people—who were mostly standing around looking bored and dignified—showed any self-confidence, fluidity, and harmony again.

The bell rang, and the children streamed inside and up the stairs. The littlest ones were quick to notice any gap where they could slip ahead in the crowd. Some of the bigger ones just pushed their way through with little regard for anyone, but their steps were less certain, and from time to time one of them would miss a step and fall.

| 4 |

Harriet's Commentary

"I'm always fascinated to see how preteens suddenly walk differently. If you look closely, it always seems as if their bones were getting in the way and making their movements awkward. It's more pronounced in some than it is in others, and usually worse in the boys than it is in the girls," Harriet commented.

"So *that's* it! I wondered why my kids seemed to be stumbling and falling so often," said Suzanne. The two women walked into the faculty lounge.

"It's exactly what the devil in the Paradise play is talking about when he says, 'They've fallen into the world of sin.' As their limbs get longer with each growth spurt, gravity's effect on the body increases because of the increase in leverage. Young teens have to adjust to these changes in leverage, and they're working on mastering them whenever they walk, jump, or run around. While they're practicing, sometimes it works and sometimes it doesn't. But do you know what that process is really all about?" Harriet paused.

"The laws of leverage teach them to think in terms of cause and effect, don't they?" responded Suzanne. "Isn't the way someone walks an image of mastering the principle of cause and effect?" "Well, yes, but most people won't know what you're talking about if you say that how your students walk reflects a mental process of coming to grips with cause and effect. However, you can point out that the students who are already interested in causative relationships tend to be the ones who are tall and thin and awkward in their movements. They're usually boys, and boys are generally more clumsy than girls. Their talent for drawing crooked lines is also related to their awkward gait; it's another instance of cause and effect—if I hold the pencil this way, the line comes out crooked, but if I hold it that way, it comes out straight. Your students were totally with it when you were demonstrating that.

"The second part of your 'sermon' this morning was all about cause and effect, too. If you had spoken like that a year ago, the children would have simply heard the words without any real understanding of the cause-and-effect relationship, and your humorous introduction would have glossed over a problem that's actually very serious. A year or two ago, you would have had to impress on the children how this incident affected you personally—presenting it artistically and sincerely, of course. But now that they're preteens, you have to do just the opposite, namely show that you're not touched by it, which you did by using humor. Humor always rises above any problem. If we were to give free rein to our subjective emotions in cases like this and react with anger, despair, or any kind of personal involvement, the young folks would listen, but they would almost certainly respond negatively.

"There's a major difficulty here, because of course both their parents and their class teacher have been working with the children since long before the preteen phase and have gotten used to showing the children what's right and what's wrong in terms of their own personal pleasure or displeasure. It's been the downfall of many parents and teachers that they go right on doing that. But at this stage, anyone who works with the youngsters has to make a conscious effort to change tactics and resort to reasoning instead. That's the only way to relate to our students appropriately so that they will learn to relate to their surroundings in the right way, and it's the secret of how to get them interested in the world around them. I can still see how attentive they were when you drew lines that kept on turning out crooked. The crooked line, the effect, was there in front of them, but where was the cause?

"But to get back to your little sermon on how to behave in traffic, I could imagine that you would still want to do it somewhat differently if you had to do it again. Do you know what I mean?"

Suzanne nodded. "I simply told my students how I saw things, and that was the wrong approach. Since they're supposed to be learning how to think for themselves, I should have asked them to volunteer something about what is expected of them in traffic and what they expect of other people in that situation. I was still presenting my thoughts on the subject and asking the kids to swallow them whole. Is that what you mean?"

Harriet smiled. "Learned your lesson well, haven't you? But let's not forget that we also have to look at the parents' side of things. You have to make some home visits and get ready for that parent-teacher meeting."

Suzanne groaned. "I knew you were going to bring that up. But before we get into that, could you tell me your impressions of the lesson itself?"

"Of course, but before I forget, let me just comment on your use of music in class. The singing was very nice, but soon you'll be running into problems—the boys' voices are going to start to change, and more and more of them will be reluctant to participate. However, music is extremely important for that age group, so you can't solve the problem by simply giving up singing as the boys start to drop out. I suggest you switch over to instruments, preferably recorders. In my experience, it's best to use pentatonic recorders in the first two grades, soprano recorders in grades three through five, and alto recorders, which are a bit bigger and deeper in pitch, from grade six on. There are so many arrangements available nowadays, you'll still find plenty of interesting pieces to challenge seventh graders.

"You'll notice that the recorders get longer as you go up through the grades. That's right in line with how the youngsters are starting to breathe more deeply. It's typical of the second seven-year period that breathing and blood circulation are constantly clashing, and with recorders or other wind instruments you can bring it all back into harmony again. Getting recorders out and putting them away again is no big deal—not like the stringed instruments that are better reserved for orchestra—so you can easily play for a bit first thing every morning. You'll need to work with the parents, though, to make sure that the youngsters are practicing at home every day.

"After that, you did recitation. May I ask why you chose that particular parable?"

Suzanne gave it some thought. "Well, after the shoplifting incident, the theme of good and evil was sort of in the air. As soon as the class can recite it fairly artistically, I'm going to ask them to formulate that conversation in their own words and see if they can express the thought that evil is one aspect of a living whole, like the ax handle cut out of the living trunk of the tree. I suspect that some of them will experience their petty thievery and sneakiness as tending in the direction of evil, but it might not be possible for them to realize it by looking at the incident directly. This example, which doesn't have anything to do with shoplifting on the face of it, might do some groundbreaking to allow them to get some insight into what they did."

"Hmmm," said Harriet. "I hope it actually works out that way."

"Why? What do *you* think is going to happen?"

"If the children figure out what you're up to, it's going to backfire; it will simply turn them off. But you'll notice that quickly enough.

"One more question, Suzanne: Why did you start by looking at the geometric figures they had drawn, instead of with the thread patterns?"

"That's something I came to in the course of this block. When we first started doing geometry this year, the children were all enthusiastic about the beautiful forms and were eager to do the drawings themselves. Unfortunately, though, not all of them have stuck to it with the same enthusiasm. Some of them have become much less careful with their drawings than they were in the beginning, and their enthusiasm has gone up in smoke. The very ones who really need to do something like precise geometric constructions are the ones who get restless and inattentive and don't cooperate. It didn't work to go on doing drawings all the time. I had to look for something else, and the thread patterns were what I came up with. I thought they just might help a few of the boys become a bit more skillful with their hands." "Do you remember the sarcastic comment from that one smart aleck?" asked Harriet. "'Oh jeez, how exciting. . . . '? That may have been a warning of resistance to come, and if so, it's because he thinks the way he's being called upon is too one- sided; there's some aspect of his mind that isn't being addressed. Like the others who aren't really participating anymore, he needs to have his attention drawn to something more than just the beauty of the forms you're drawing; they have been going in that direction for too long already, and that's why you don't seem to get any further with it. They need to have their thinking challenged." Harriet pulled out a geometry textbook. "See this little equilateral triangle? It contains a certain number of rhombuses and trapezoids. First, for the girls, you explain what a rhombus is in very graphic terms—show them the suit of diamonds from a pack of cards. And a trapezoid is the shape made by a circus trapeze and the ropes suspending it from the big top. Then, primarily for the boys, you'll want to describe these forms in geometrical terms. After that, you can show them this drawing and ask them to see how many different triangles, rhombuses, and trapezoids they can find in it.

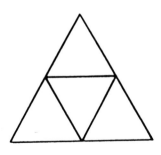

If you then go on to look at one really beautiful example of geometric form-drawing, you will have approached the lesson from both sides."

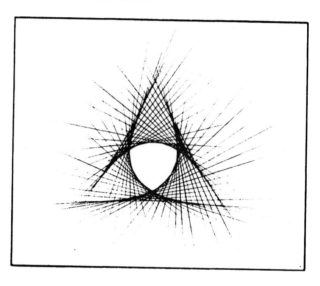

Harriet continued, "You see, when you are looking at a beautiful geometric form, you're living totally in the impression of it; when you're caught up in enjoying that beautiful form, you're more out there in what you're looking at than you are inside yourself. On the other hand, when you're trying to discover the laws governing a rhombus or a trapezoid, or finding out how many of those shapes are contained in a drawing like this, then you're being inwardly active. When you're actively thinking, you're more inside yourself.

"In the first instance, the students are drawn out into the periphery, and in the second, they're more active within themselves. That is very important. When we admire something beautiful, that's easy on our souls, because our ego is outside of us. Thinking, or conceiving of something in terms of natural laws, is 'hard'; it takes a certain effort, and that pulls our ego back in. That's what's behind it if we say a math problem is easy, hard, or even too hard.

"If you use both of these aspects alternately in your lessons, then the class won't get too dull and 'hard to reach'; and they won't get dreamy and inattentive either. You're holding the tiller, and you have to make sure the wind is always in the sails; if you just keep going from one beautiful form to the next, eventually you'll be becalmed."

"So I shouldn't have introduced the thread patterns, after all?"

"They're fine, but you have to use them in connection with something that requires mental effort. Don't forget, a balanced lesson needs to include both breathing in and breathing out. If you take that into account, the subject teachers will also have fewer difficulties with your class. As it is, you have to bring external pressure to bear to keep things in balance, and you're lucky if the ship doesn't tip over."

"Thank you," said Suzanne. "That was very helpful. But wasn't there something else, still? Didn't I see you taking notes while I was praising some of their drawings and criticizing others?"

Harriet searched through her notes. "Oh yes, it was the comparisons that concerned me. You certainly did keep the whole class in mind. Of course, evaluation, either positive or negative, is a natural part of teaching, and your students expect to get a clear assessment of their work from you. But you have to be very careful not to damage the social fabric of the class when you do it. Don't say, 'So-and-so did a better job than any of the rest of you.' Instead, say something like, 'So-and-so did a good job and set a very good example for the rest of you. Congratulations, all of you, on having learned so much from him!'

"My experience with criticism, on the other hand, has always been that it's better to say it in private if the person in question is more than twelve years old, or actually even younger than that. Otherwise, the students whose work you've criticized may try to bolster their self-confidence by either putting on a show of indifference or becoming uncooperative. In either case, your criticism probably won't bring about any improvement in their work. Anyway, for you the most important thing is to find out why the youngsters aren't doing acceptable work. Isn't there enough peace and quiet at home? Aren't they eating a balanced diet? Are there any health problems, any difficulties with their friends on the way home from school? Once you've discovered where the problem lies, you'll know where to direct your efforts to help. And if you're really sure they're just being lazy, you can always tell them (in private, of course), 'We're going to have a look at your drawings tomorrow.' But having said that, don't you dare forget!"

"And how would you have reacted to the business with the chair?"

"I just heard it crash; I didn't really see what was going on," said Harriet.

"Neither did I; that's why I didn't do anything more than get rid of the pieces. But later I'll ask that girl and the one sitting next to her what happened."

"I think that's the right way to react. If you try to get into all kinds of investigations after two hours of main lesson, you are not going to get anywhere at all. The youngsters simply need a break by then. And when in doubt, it's always better to underreact rather than overreact. A child who is treated unfairly at this age will remember it for a lifetime. When they're just on the verge of adolescence, you have to weigh every single word you say, because if you react in the wrong way, it might just turn the whole class against you, especially if it's a class dominated by girls. Girls of this age are much more self-confident than boys, and they're going to let any teacher know it.

"But I don't think you should just let the incident slide. Try to learn the motive behind it—was it simply an accident, or carelessness, or was it premeditated mischief? That will determine what you need to do about it. But whatever you do, do it from the point of view of setting the stage or painting the scenery; you want to present your young 'actors' with an exact depiction of the circumstances they were involved in. Hold it up to them as an image, so they can take a good look at themselves. That's a prerequisite for objectively distancing yourself from what you've done so that you can assess it. If you can carry out the investigation like this, it can already remedy the situation to quite an extent, even without punishment.

"But I've been doing so much talking!" Harriet apologized. "I really am an old-fashioned schoolmarm at heart. But how does it feel when you stand in front of the class now? Any different?"

"The main thing is that I don't feel like I have to deal with it all alone anymore," Suzanne acknowledged. "That gives me courage to get on with my job, and I'm really grateful. I'm much more clear on a lot of things already— for instance, you can't always stick to the same technique even if it has always worked for you before. Strict discipline, for example, or reciting in unison, or the way I told stories and talked about them afterward, among other things. I guess even the best of teachers would run into problems if they thought they could just go on teaching in the same old way even though the kids have entered a new developmental phase meanwhile. When that happens, the students and the teacher take off in different directions.

"I thought of something else, too. In the beginning, I always used to kind of cling to my own inadequacies and think they were worse than they really are. For a long time I thought I'd gotten over that, especially when the children were really receptive and happy with my teaching. Recently, though, I started to get depressed again. I really blew it trying to explain three-step problems in arithmetic, and then I felt so inadequate I thought I just couldn't go on. It's really strange, you know; just when your students get into adolescence and their emotional life is suddenly a big deal and causes all kinds of hassles for them, you suddenly get oversensitive yourself and all your old faults show up again, big as life. On the other hand, it kind of wakes you up to have to experience them again. I guess that's the positive side of the whole thing, isn't it?"

Harriet nodded. "That's exactly why self-education is so important for anyone who has to see youngsters through adolescence. But it would help if you could speak to the parents about what's going on and tell them that something new is dawning in their children's emotional life. After all, it's not just sexual maturity they're approaching, it's real earthly maturity, adulthood on all fronts. And that's really a kind of new birth."

Suzanne had to bring the conversation to an end. "I have to get back to class now, but we can talk about that next time, ok? I'm really going to need your help with that parents' meeting."

SUGGESTED READING:

Erich Gabert, *Educating the Adolescent*, Anthroposophic Press, 1988.

Erich Katz, *Recorder Playing: A New and Comprehensive Method*, Carl Van Roy Publishing Co., 1970.

Rudolf Steiner, *Balance in Teaching*, Mercury Press, 1982.

Rudolf Steiner, *The Education of the Child*, Anthroposophic Press, 1976.

Rudolf Steiner, *The Spiritual Ground of Education*, Anthroposophical Publishing Co., London, 1947.

| 5 |

The Transformation around Age Twelve

"Let's pick up from where we left off last time, " said Harriet at their next meeting. "If you look at what children are like before and after this transition to the preteen stage, I'm sure you'll notice a big difference. What comes to mind?"

Suzanne considered for a moment. "Before, the children were full of love for their parents and teachers and for everything around them in nature, and it carried over to everything I presented in class. They needed that kind of immediate connection to make them feel comfortable and secure, and their happiness was totally dependent on this loving way of relating to their surroundings."

"You're absolutely right. Younger children have a legitimate, if self-centered, need for that kind of love, and it encompasses everything they perceive and feel until they turn twelve, more or less. But what happens to this active affective aspect after that? What is it directed to now?"

Suzanne didn't have to think long about that. "It's as if their attachment to adults has simply been wiped out. Sometimes they get defensive if you so much as put a hand on their shoulder. But they can also be drawn to people with an interest and intensity that just wasn't there before—when they make new friends, for instance. New friendships can develop out of the blue and be very intense. On the other hand, they seem to have lost interest in their school subjects." She paused for a moment. "No, that's not totally true, but their interest is different. They're hungry for experiences, for strong sense impressions that arouse either their disgust or their craving for more. They seem to be torn between these two extremes, and everything is reduced to likes and dislikes. And they almost pounce on sense impressions to satisfy their craving to the full." Suzanne was silent for a moment.

"What are you thinking about?" asked Harriet.

"How important seeing and hearing become for people that age. Suddenly it's as if they couldn't do without an awful lot of noise. One mother told me how her son tied an empty tin can to the end of a string and pulled it around just to hear the noise. Then he and a friend got a whole bunch of tin cans and tied them to a parked car. They hid and waited until the driver came back and pulled away from the curb. The racket was enough to make you plug your ears! And the sound of breaking glass is equally fascinating to them, not to mention noisy engines and tapes played at full volume. All that's incredibly important all of a sudden. And they're just as hungry for visual impressions— photographs, posters, magazines, television, movies, video, disco lights—you name it. These impressions are so strong nothing else can compete.

"It's the same with the other senses, too. Once someone in the class put a smoldering shoelace under the French teacher's desk before class. What a stink! They're eager to smell things like ammonia, gasoline, tar, exhaust fumes—

and then they make a big deal out of it with loud expressions of disgust. The girls are somewhat more subtle, I must admit. They're into perfume and makeup—things to enhance their own sensual appeal. And both the boys and the girls tend to go for extremes in taste—things that are very sour, spicy, or sweet. They seem to be ravenous for sensory experiences of all kinds." Suzanne hesitated, recalling a dream she had had recently. Her students had been roller-skating in a huge space filled with movie posters, executing fancy steps to the sound of subdued pop music. "Doesn't this craving for intense impressions and adventure tend to draw people into intoxication and even addiction?"

"You're right not to underestimate the temptations people their age are facing," Harriet responded. "All too often they do lead to drug abuse. But don't get all worked up about it right away, because that's only one side of the picture. What you have to understand is that at this stage the only way youngsters have access to the phenomena around them is from the outside. When they were younger, their way of perceiving was much more inward. I'll bet that, except for the very precocious ones, they were all willing to go along with it when you asked them to paint a forest of evergreens to evoke a mood of peace and reverence, or to make the eagle's feathers golden. I remember a zoology lesson with one of my classes—we'd been talking about bulls, about how strong and dangerous and full of tremendous energy they are, and one of the boys said to me that he knew bulls didn't give milk, but if they did, it would be red! But now they take things literally; milk has to be white, the eagle's feathers are not golden, and you'd better not paint a tree blue unless it's a blue spruce.

"Their souls are no longer so at one with the things around them; their affective energy has all pulled back into their bodies, and their eyes see only what's on the surface. Meanwhile, the urge to be at one with the outer world is still there inside as a very strong emotional impulse, and yet they can only perceive the world from outside. Somehow, they still yearn for the paradise they've lost and try to either dream or force their way back in, or else they get totally 'out of it' in fits of uncontrollable giggling. That's also typical of people of this age. Trying to establish a deeper connection, and trying in vain because they're constantly bouncing off the surface of things, is what lies behind all those vehement drives, desires, and passions of theirs.

"You're perfectly justified in seeing this as a threat to the young people's development; in certain areas preteens experience a real set-back. As young children whose senses were not yet fully developed, they were poorer in some respects but richer in their inner life, in their emotions. But now, as their senses mature, that aspect becomes poorer. Of course, there's a deeper meaning to having to come to grips with all that, just as there's a deeper meaning to the Biblical expulsion from Paradise. And it's that meaning you need to present to the parents. You can demonstrate it in terms of how their youngsters' ways of walking, talking, thinking, and experiencing their social context have changed."

Suzanne was overwhelmed by the enormity of the task. "Harriet, you're going to have to help me. There's no way I can do that on my own! I'm really dependent on your experience."

"Of course I'll help," the older woman replied. "That's why we're working together. Don't worry, we'll make sure your parents' meeting is well prepared. But I don't want to get away from the topic of the senses just yet. You gave such a vivid description earlier of what's going on there, you obviously have a good grasp of it.

"Seeing and hearing were the first senses you singled out, weren't they, Suzanne? All we're doing with the Waldorf curriculum is educating the children's senses, and now, in sixth grade, there's a special focus on those two senses. In the course of this year, you will be introducing the study of physics with lesson blocks on optics and acoustics. When you study optics, you bring in black and white sheets of paper and have the students look at them through prisms so they'll observe not only the contrast but also how the edges take on color where dark and light areas meet. You're addressing their senses, not loudly or forcibly, but as a riddle to be answered—how do those rainbow edges come about? You're calling on their mental alertness; instead of simply heaping sense impressions on top of sense impressions, you ask them to reflect quietly on those impressions. They're forced to engage in some inner activity to try to figure out what makes the edges colored. Once the youngsters have discovered that the prism displaces the surfaces slightly, so that light and dark areas overlap each other, the next question is, when do we see red and when do we see blue?

"Then you take a flashlight and hold layers of wax paper in front of the bulb—the more layers, the redder it gets. Some of your students will probably take a flashlight to bed with them and try it out under the covers. What do you know—it works when you stretch the sheet over the light, too! In class, you fill a glass jar with water and shine a light through it. Meanwhile, you make the water go cloudy by slowly adding liquid soap. Depending on the angle of your line of sight, the cloud of soap may look blue, but when you're looking directly into the light, it's orange. What does that suggest about how red sunsets and the blue sky of midday come about? You stimulate more and more questions in the minds of the young people and lead them to experience quietly and inwardly that blue is lit-up darkness, while red is what happens to the light when it penetrates darkness or opacity. They start to experience red as the active aspect of light and blue as its passive side, to experience red as courageous and blue as restrained, quiet, and reverent. The initial sense impression has been transformed through the deliberate and conscious process of coming to understand it, and grasping the essence of a sensory phenomenon leads to a moral conclusion."

Suzanne had been following Harriet's discourse with enthusiasm and a considerable sense of relief at being shown how to proceed in class. Here was something she could really sink her teeth into—a way to transform the impressions the class was experiencing so strongly and generate a constructive kind of energy. Relating to colors in this way would make the children's body-bound impressions receptive to sensing and reenlivening the very essence of the different colors and would open up totally new possibilities for their painting sessions, too.

"When you do acoustics, you will also be able to demonstrate how the sense of hearing relates to what is inherent in sound," Harriet continued. "If you construct a scale by shortening the string of a monochord and then compare the lengths of the different pitches to the string-length of the tonic pitch, you'll find a mathematical confirmation of what your ears are hearing—if you divide the string-length of the tonic by the string-length of a second pitch, it will come out even if the two notes harmonize. For instance, the tonic-to-octave proportion is two to one. Dissonant intervals, however, yield fractions that just go on forever when you try to divide them out. It can be a real therapeutic revelation for the students to learn how well their ears can 'measure'. This will help them acquire a healthy respect for their extremely finely differentiated organs of hearing. They begin to realize that when they hear a scale, they 'hear' laws that are also present in the very way their bodies are put together. Basically, in all that deafening noise they enjoy so much, they're only trying to grasp the essence of sound and pitch although, in fact, turning up the volume actually works counter to what they're looking for.

"Then you can go on to talk about damage to the sense organs through overly strong sense impressions. Read them some reports by doctors. What is it that actually forms our ears or our eyes? What is the effect of hard rock, TV, video, and disco lighting?

"From now on, all your instruction is directed toward educating their senses, and not only their eyes and ears. The starting point for you as a teacher is the riddle that lies behind each and every sense impression. You'll need to carefully consider the questions you ask in class—are they calculated to enlarge upon sense impressions, transform them, and evoke a sense of wonder at the process?

"Presenting vivid sense impressions in terms of a riddle, and then 'solving' the riddle by becoming conscious of the process—those are two complementary aspects of your lesson. The combination should subdue the intensity of your students' sensory experience and work to bring about a balance that can serve as the basis for building self-confidence. In the course of this process, you as a teacher will change from being an authority to being a helpmate, from someone who commands to someone whose role is to point out more and more riddles and questions inherent in our sense-perceptible environment."

Suzanne went over the whole process in her mind once more, then reached for a pencil and drew a couple of quick sketches:

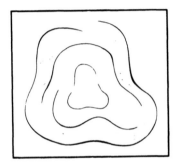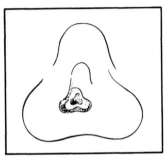

"It works like this, doesn't it, Harriet? Here on the left is what it's like for children under twelve—they're surrounded by their parents and teachers and direct all their feelings and will-impulses out toward them. In the sketch on the right, slightly older children are here in the middle—they incorporate into themselves everything that used to stream out toward the periphery; they're separating themselves from their surroundings and becoming self-aware in their senses."

"I think you've grasped the idea," agreed Harriet, "and the process can be compared to waking up in the morning. Before age twelve, children are wrapped up in a kind of cloud; through it, they experience the world imaginatively. On the threshold of puberty, however, they undergo a waking process, and what used to be outside in the 'cloud' moves inside and becomes part of their own body. When this process is complete, sexual maturity has been achieved. Then the youngsters perceive everything exactly, but don't really know what they are perceiving. It's like being on a trip and waking up in a strange place one morning—you see everything clearly, but it takes a while before you realize where you are. But you do *want* to know where you are, and that's a good healthy instinct that can be cultivated and can develop into a real interest in the world around you. People often call sleep the little brother of death, and it would be just as right to call waking up the little sister of birth. It's much easier to understand what happens when a person is born if you imagine it as waking up to find yourself in surroundings you don't know anything about yet."

"There's something I still don't quite understand. Where's the individuality in all this? What about the students as individuals?" asked Suzanne.

Harriet hesitated. "This is going to sound very roundabout, but I'd like to try to answer your question by describing two different approaches to main lesson in the subjects we just talked about. Suppose one teacher is doing optics and does lots and lots of experiments and insists on very neat and accurate entries in the main-lesson books, but asks almost no questions. Something is missing because the students aren't really challenged to reflect on what they have seen. On the other hand, something is also missing if the teacher doesn't insist on precise and beautiful drawings, and runs through the experiments very quickly in order to be able to spend most of the time talking about them. That teacher's theory is that the main thing is for the material to be digested and that it happens through talking about it in class. In both cases, an important process has been left out. Seeing that process through—and this is where your question comes in—means making sure that the students' perceptions were accurate in the first place. Checking the students' main-lesson books for accurate drawings and reports of experiments is a good way to check up on that.

But the second step is to make sure that these perceptions undergo a higher, more objective cognitive process, a process through which we learn something about the phenomena themselves instead of simply reacting personally and subjectively to our impressions. If we only get as far as subjective reaction, we don't learn anything about the things themselves. Each student must draw the connection between his or her perceptions, which are very limited in scope, and the broader and more objective conclusions that can be drawn from them. It wakes people up to go through that process. Afterward, their eyes see more keenly and take more pleasure in what they see, and their individual effort is what makes the main-lesson books good."

"Oh," said Suzanne, picking up where Harriet left off, "Now I see why adolescents are so frequently compared to ships in a storm. It's as if all those impressions were crashing in on them like waves breaking, but. . . ."

". . . that's why young people really don't want to be addressed with regard to where they're at," Harriet went on, rubbing it in a bit. "If we speak to where they are now, it only makes them worse. On the other hand, if we address them with regard to how they would actually like to be, we can get them on the right track. This applies to everyone involved in the children's upbringing and education—teachers, parents, and everyone else. But it's no longer acceptable for adults to be authority figures. We have to realize we're treading on holy ground."

"And what did you think of my diagram?" inquired Suzanne.

"Well, there's something very true in it, but like any diagram, it doesn't quite give the whole picture. You have to realize, for instance, that girls don't react to this waking-up process the same way boys do. I remember a colleague saying to me once that boys are always on the lookout for sense impressions, while girls are much more concerned with the kind of impression they can make themselves. That accounts for the makeup, the flirting, and being able to turn on the tears at will. Take it one step further, and their self-assertiveness turns into stormy protest. Girls stand up for themselves; they're going to let you know what's what. Imagine the tirade at home if you've established a dress code for the class, for instance. There stands the girl, straight as an arrow, telling you off *in absentia*. 'I'm not going to take that lying down! I'll show that teacher! It's *my* face and *my* body and I can wear whatever I want!' You can feel the blood welling up in these seething emotions. In general, the circulatory system is much more strongly at work in adolescent girls than in boys."

"And how should parents react to that kind of thing, Harriet?"

"In this case, it's best if the girl's mother or whoever happens to be on the receiving end shows some polite interest and asks a few tactful questions without taking sides. And then her mother suddenly remembers she's lost her car keys or something and turns away, literally and figuratively, and leaves her daughter to cool off by herself. That's the right way to handle the situation, because it lets the girl let off steam, and eventually she'll notice on her own that it wasn't really worth such a fuss."

"Sounds good," laughed Suzanne. "And if it were a boy? Then what?"

"Boys are generally much more shy. You told me yourself about those young pranksters watching from a safe hiding place. Girls would come out and laugh in the face of the dumbfounded driver, but boys aren't that sure of themselves. For instance, if there are a couple of boys organizing a totally harmless bike race and you ask them what they're doing, the mere fact that someone has been watching what's been going on may be enough to embarrass them, and you'll see them turn red in the face. Unless there's some compelling reason, you should avoid asking a boy what he's doing, just as you should avoid stepping on a girl's emotional turf. In both cases, it's best to look right past it. You need to realize, for instance, that if some boys break something, they only come to their senses enough to know what they've done after the fact. It's not a question of bad will, and in most cases they're already somewhat uncomfortable about having done it, so you should respond with a bit of humor instead of taking it too seriously. That way, you'll let the boys realize by themselves that they've done something stupid, but without risking losing their sympathy. On the other hand, if you overreact, they're going to be afraid of you and stop liking you.

"Another thing we have to remember about boys is that it's easy to overstimulate them with excessive impressions and demands, both at home and in school, since they're more nervous than girls. After a while, they want to withdraw and be by themselves. We have to respect that; we have to show that we understand and think it's all right. That makes it much easier for young men to develop emotional depth later on. Without it, it's possible for them to become superficial, materialistic, or even brutal."

"I see," said Suzanne, "and how would you describe the girls' emotional life?"

Harriet was ready for that one. "You can see the excessive strength of a girl's emotions in how very up front she can be. That can express itself in outrage, anger, or hatred. On the other hand, girls can also be tender and devoted to the point of losing themselves. All this is almost elemental in its intensity; it's like an outburst of some force of nature, and whatever gets in the way can either be smashed to bits or praised to the skies. These sensations are like a dry sponge soaking up the core of a girl's being, her personal center. That's what makes it so difficult for girls of that age to enter into real relationships with others.

"It's different with boys, though. They haven't found their center at all yet, and that's why they don't get so wrapped up in their own emotions or get so vehement about them. The tragedy of the boys is that they don't really know what to do with themselves, except to stand there helplessly with their hands in their pockets, trying to reveal as little of themselves as possible. They run the risk of simply copping out, of turning into cowards. To put it graphically, we just bounce off the girls' hard shell, but boys are like a raw egg. As I said once before, that's why you have to weigh every single word carefully before you speak, and that's not easy."

Suzanne was silent, trying to digest this conversation. She thought back to last year, to the botany block she had chosen to start the school year. The children had been totally with it, painting the tender, cheerful, virginal birch with dabs of yellow, blue, and green; imagining the weeping willow with its twigs touching the water as a young widow; painting the oak tree, that stalwart old battle-ax, in red and brown and green; following her into the somber stillness of the melancholy forest of evergreens. . . . They had all been so eager to please, so open to her suggestions as they worked on the pictures and text of their main-lesson books. As pure and innocent as the plants reaching for the sun—that's what they had been like inside. Then Suzanne summoned up an image of the class as it was now—self-willed, awkward, troublesome and difficult to guide. Something had gotten into them that stirred up their emotions, something that could go in the direction of either longing or resistance, although it was sometimes more pronounced and sometimes less so.

"What a contrast," thought Suzanne. "But it's wrong to even wish that I could hold them back. They're trying to get on with it, to move on and develop new forces, and forward is the only way to go, even if these new forces are all mixed up with passions and longings. I can only hope these youngsters will eventually find the courage to face themselves and tell truth from untruth, to acquire the strength that is as powerful and as selfless as the red of a rose."

In that instant, Suzanne experienced all her own concerns and shortcomings like stones on her path, obstacles she had to climb around or over. "I guess I have to learn to look myself in the eye, too," she confessed to herself. But she felt considerable resistance to her own critical self-searching and had to admit that she would not be able to simply get rid of her own shortcomings just like that. "I'll have to learn to accept them and deal with them," she thought, "to take them as they are but still to work on them and to maintain my self-respect. That will help me understand my students."

Harriet seemed to read her thoughts. "Working on ourselves is a prerequisite for teachers," she said carefully. "There's always a certain amount of grace involved when children turn out all right. That we can count on that grace is what gives us hope."

Suzanne nodded. Harriet pulled out a single handwritten page. "Here, read this. I treasure it because a girl in one of my classes gave it to me at her eighth-grade graduation. You see, once these young folks have put in their time battling the waves of one-sidedness, they acquire the right organs of perception to be able to see through their own shells. Then it's as if the young individualities were pecking their way out like little birds out of their shells, until finally they stand there saying, 'Here I am!' It'll happen with your class, too. Go on, read it!"

Thanks to Life

Thank you, life, giving
for giving me laughter and tears—
now I know happiness;
now I know despair.

Thank you, life,
for giving me love and hatred—
now I know joy;
now I know pain.

Thank you, life,
for giving me fire and ice
light and shadow,
waking and sleep;

for giving me
delight at the sight of a newly hatched bird,
and sadness at its dying.

Thank you, life,
for giving yourself
to me.

SUGGESTED READING:

Willi Aeppli, *Rudolf Steiner Education and the Developing Child*, Anthroposophic Press, 1987.

Rudolf Steiner, *Soul Economy and Waldorf Education*, Anthroposophic Press, 1987.

Rudolf Steiner, *Deeper Insights into Education: The Waldorf School Approach*, Anthroposophic Press, 1983.

Rudolf Steiner, *Waldorf Education for Adolescents, Supplementary Course: The Upper School*, Kolisko Archives Publications (Michael Hall School), 1980.

Rudolf Steiner, *The Kingdom of Childhood*, Anthroposophic Press.

| *6* |

The Parent-Teacher Meeting

"Good evening, everyone! It is not easy for me to introduce tonight's meeting, due to recent events that are grounds for concern for all of us. Above all, we have reason to be concerned about the recent series of department store thefts. Before we get into that, though, I think it would be helpful to step back and look at the larger picture.

It was more than two years ago—almost three years ago by now—that this class crossed the Rubicon and entered a new phase of childhood around age nine. This was a very decisive event, and here and there it provoked crises, the first real difficulties I had experienced with the class. When we talked about it back then, we noted that the last remnants of the power of imitation had disappeared. Until then, the children had been eager to participate in everything going on around them; their will had inextricably united them with their surroundings. Now, however, this force no longer carried them; the will at work in the power of imitation was no longer enough to bridge the gap between them and their environment. But meanwhile a new element was appearing, namely, an intensified capacity for experiencing things. It expressed itself in their feelings and was beginning to replace the old bridge. It began to work just as we were doing a lesson block on the story of Creation.

"In line with the loss the children had experienced in their world as their capacity for imitation faded, the first thing we did was to imagine away everything that human beings had created on earth. Next we imagined away everything God had created. Then I asked the class where everything was when there was nothing there yet, and the answer they came up with was that everything was still with God. We then heard the story of the creation of everything that exists on earth. We heard how God created human beings last of all, breathing his own living breath into Adam. The children could experience the divinity living both within them and all around them. They experienced the revelation of God in the rushing wind and the lapping water, in the depth of the sky and the warmth of the sun. Every little bug and flower bore witness to the Creator.

"The following year, we studied animals as they relate to human beings, and I could see how strongly the children's feelings were still engaged in experiencing everything around them. For example, with a bare minimum of prompting they could feel their way into an animal and describe what it was like from the inside. I asked them what kind of an animal would come about if we could free our seeing and hearing and all our other senses from the heaviness of our body so that they could soar up into the air, and they described how light a bird felt with the wind in its feathers and how it tested its balance as it circled up above; how it could see and hear everything going on down below.

"Then they discovered that digesting, gathering its forces together, and being placid and persistent were what made the large and heavy cow; and that flaming enthusiasm and courage were what the lion presents to us. It didn't take much at all for the children to experience the cow's heaviness, the bird's lightness, or the lion's warmth and courage.

Even in fifth grade, it was still possible for the children to enter wholeheartedly into their environment. When they looked at a birch tree, it was like a happy young girl dancing around in her Sunday dress; the dark evergreens were very serious thinkers ruminating on the mysteries of the distant past. The birch craved light, while the pines liked to stand close together so they could shade each other. The children were still experiencing the essence of things in pictorial form. During these middle years of childhood, they were wonderfully devoted to the plants and animals they learned about and also wonderfully devoted to their classmates, their parents, and their teachers. It was a marvelously harmonious time when it was possible for anything, anything at all, to come to life in their young souls. They were filled with a sense of the divine origin of every living thing.

"Now that they are in sixth grade, however, that time is definitely over, and there's a new wind blowing. The children are different now, right down to the way they look. But what is it that's changed so much?" Suzanne had actually meant that as a rhetorical question, but immediately some of the mothers and fathers were ready with comments and opinions.

Pam's mother was the first to speak up: "Not too long ago, you did that poem about the origin of evil with the class: 'The world comes from God, and God can only have the good within Himself. How then can evil men come from the good?' Until now, our children have been living in God's own creation, and they saw that it was good. But now things have changed; they don't take that for granted any more. Recently my daughter said to me, 'In some ways people are really wicked, aren't they, Mom?' I was surprised, and asked why she thought that. Pam hesitated for a while, but then she said, 'You have no idea how bad our class is.' I asked if she meant the shoplifting, and she just nodded. I think she's been thinking about it a lot."

Soon other parents joined in. "Our Matthew would never talk about anything like that if we left it up to him," said another mother. "He just withdraws into himself as soon as we mention it. He's really trying to avoid the issue."

"You can tell, though, that the class has suffered socially because of the shoplifting. They keep splitting up into opposing groups and rival cliques," said Michael's father. "I really don't see how it can go on like that."

"It's really noticeable how rude our daughter's gotten," said Melissa's mother. "She didn't used to be like that at all. Just a couple days ago she took a book—not a big thick one, fortunately—and hit her little sister over the head with it. And when I intervened, she put on a big show and said she was going to hit harder next time!"

"It's just the opposite with our son Jeff," interjected another mother. "When the kids get into an argument, all I have to do is say, 'What's going on here? What did you do?' and he's offended and disappears into his room. Not a trace of opposition there. He is so easily offended sometimes, so oversensitive. And then he just pulls back into his shell like a snail, and it takes days before we can even talk to each other again. I just don't know what to do about it!"

Several others nodded their agreement. "They just don't obey any more. If you want them to do something, the first thing they say is 'Why?'" "You're right; they have no respect for authority anymore," another father picked up where the last left off. "That's perfectly clear in our son's case, at least. You should hear Mike complain at home: 'Do you know how she talks to us? First it's "children," and then it's "dear children." What does she think we are, babies or something? Or is she practicing to take a first grade again?'"

"They're developing a very strong sense of justice, though. Holly's been getting terribly upset about the fact that all the children—students, I mean—have to go outside at recess. 'How come we always have to go out, while those teachers get to sit around in the teachers' room and drink coffee? I'm really fed up with it!'"

"On the other hand, they've gotten much more shy in some ways," another mother volunteered. "Our daughter Kristin would really rather not be touched at all anymore. And last time we went shopping for a sweater, she wanted one two sizes too big so her breasts wouldn't show. It's not just that they've gotten rude, they've also started to get embarrassed. Their feelings have really changed."

"And you have to watch every single word you say to them," another woman commented. "A couple of evenings ago, Lori was taking forever with her homework because she was goofing around with her sister, and I finally said to her, 'Will you quit yakking and get down to work? You're always yakking!' 'What do you mean, always? I'm not always yakking!' And then she turned around and went to her father: 'Daddy, can you help me? I can't do these problems!'"

"Well, at least I don't have to complain about how Paul does his homework, but I wish he'd do as good a job at keeping his room looking halfway decent. What a mess! And he's always losing things. 'Uh oh, what did I do with my key?' 'There it is, right under your nose!' 'Oh, yeah,' says he, as he grabs it on his way out the door. Right now he can't even find things if they're staring him in the face."

Another mother broke in, "Besides the shoplifting, what I'm most concerned about are the sexual incidents going on in class. I don't really know what's happening, but Sarah says it gets so bad, she's ashamed to go to class!"

Bob's mother, who was older and more experienced than some of the others, spoke up: "We mustn't make the mistake of taking everything our children tell us at face value, though. What we've been talking about is typical teenage behavior—getting all riled up and taking sides and getting into rivalries with each other; evading the issue and having their feelings hurt; and being just plain rude, too. That's what this transitional phase is all about. Even when it comes to sexual difficulties, I don't think we can simply look at things from the point of view of adults. These kids are on the verge of sexual maturity, and it's new territory for them in a lot of different ways. They don't really know how to cope with what they're experiencing, let alone talk about it without using obscenities. In my experience, it's best if you talk quite openly with them. 'Mom, what's a hooker?' my son asked not too long ago. We talked about what she does and what her reasons for doing it might be, and he was very quiet for a while, thinking about it. The worst thing we can do is try to keep things secret or avoid certain topics because they make us feel uncomfortable. I think we just ought to go ahead and talk about whatever it is when we notice something is wrong. From that point of view, it would also be really helpful if you would make a point of calling us to tell us what's gone on at school, Suzanne.

"We have two children who are grown up already, so we have some experience with teenagers. For instance, all my children have started to complain about my cooking just at this age. 'Yuck, macaroni and cheese again?' Or 'How come we always have rice?' I'm afraid I did take it personally to begin with, as a criticism of my cooking, or even as ingratitude. But when I saw it happening a third time with our youngest son, it made me stop and think, and I came to the conclusion—obvious as it may be— that at this age everything is a question of taste, and I don't just mean food. Having 'taste' means that people like and dislike different things, but that doesn't mean one is right and the other wrong. They're judging everything, or at least a lot of things, simply in terms of what they like and don't like. It's not just a question of food; it applies to music, dancing, clothes, and so on. One day Bob came home with this absolutely unbelievable haircut. I was too shocked to say a word at first, and before I could open my mouth he was already telling me, 'You don't understand, you don't know what's "in," you just have no taste!' And they want to wear the craziest outfits. . . .

"Uh oh, now I've lost my train of thought. Anyway, what I wanted to say was that we can't understand what our kids are telling us if we only judge it—either positively or negatively— from an adult point of view. They're going through a phase where they've lost their former taste. For the time being, they don't know what tastes good or is healthy or looks good or is acceptable to say, and so on and so forth. Their personal impressions are all they have to go by. They've actually dropped out of everything that was there before. It's different from the third-grade crisis this time because instead of just feeling vaguely apprehensive inside, they're full of raging emotions that want to get out, and they take it out on us. I've come to realize that that is just the way things go, and I can put up with it now that I don't take it personally and don't go around judging what they're doing from my grown-up point of view. After all, it doesn't really have anything to do with me personally."

One of the fathers cleared his throat and put in his point of view. "It may well be the way you describe it, Mrs. Morris, especially when you were talking about entering new territory. But I wonder how things are going to go if we just let them mouth off whenever they feel like it. In our house, we don't put up with bad manners or insolent remarks. I think it does have something to do with me, and the fact that this shoplifting has been going on has something to do with all of us. I mean, we can't just detach ourselves to the point of being mere onlookers; after all, this mess our children are in concerns us too."

It was all too easy for Suzanne to understand how Mr. Davis felt, because that was exactly how she had also assessed the situation before Harriet and others had helped her to see what was going on behind all this adolescent behavior. It was only gradually and with considerable effort that Suzanne herself was coming anywhere near Bob's mother's degree of objectivity and distance from her son—a "distance" that allowed her to be much closer to him and say much more to him than someone with Mr. Davis' attitude possibly could. Before her discussions with Harriet, however, Suzanne had found that teaching was taking such a lot out of her that she was on the verge of total exhaustion. It had been so important to her to do everything "right" that she hadn't let her students deviate from the path by even a single step. If they had, she would have seen it as a failure on her part. Now she had realized that all she could hope to do was moderate their excesses as they appeared—trying to suppress them would do no good at all. But before she could respond to Mr. Davis, another father stepped in.

"I want to bring up something else, and it has to do with how you're conducting your lessons, Suzanne. Jessica seems to have the attitude that if she can't do something, she doesn't have to worry about it. 'Never mind, she won't do anything if I don't learn it.' It seems to me that the class isn't being pressured to perform up to par. And experiencing success after having to make an effort is a real boost to anyone's morale."

One of the mothers, obviously uncomfortable with that, spoke up, "I don't want to gloss over their shoplifting or make excuses for it," she said. "They obviously need good guidance and clear standards of behavior, but they've gotten that already. As far as pressure and performance are concerned, I can't really agree with you on that point. No youngster who is put under pressure to perform by being graded and threatened with having to repeat a grade is going to do the better for it. On the contrary, our daughter has been in this school for only one year; before that she had to deal with the usual pressure of grades and the possibility of having to repeat a grade. You wouldn't believe what a burden that was to her—it was even affecting her health. But since she's been here, she's positively blossomed."

One of the other fathers came to the defense of Jessica's dad. "I don't think grades and staying back were what he was talking about, otherwise he wouldn't have sent his children to a Waldorf school in the first place. I think I feel the same way he does. I'd be glad if the kids were kept under control a bit better—especially in French class, but also in their other classes—and the class teacher needs to make more of an effort. After all, some of these youngsters will be attending other schools or going to college at some point, and that could be a rude awakening for them."

"But let's not forget that kids this age are already faced with a double challenge," said Bob Morris' mother, the woman with two grown children. "What I mean is their physical development on the one hand and having to meet the demands of school on the other. After all, none of us is very enthusiastic about having to do our best if we have a toothache or a headache or don't feel well for some other reason. And even if we can't see what's going on, puberty is making extreme demands on them as their bodies are being worked on and changed. Most girls get their first period in fifth or sixth grade. Their whole constitution is being transformed, and that already uses up a certain amount of mental and emotional energy. I don't think it's right to force them to learn at this age to the extent that was possible earlier and will be again later. Our oldest girl was a very poor student at that age, and we were really worried about her, but now she's going to college and is in very good health, and it's probably because she wasn't forced to overdo it as a young teenager."

"The children have to enjoy learning," contributed Mrs. Slater, who hadn't spoken until now. "If they do, all of their problems can be solved—including puberty!"

By now, all of the parents had spoken their mind and were wondering how Suzanne would respond.

"I want to thank all of you for the many and varied points of view you've expressed. On the one hand, some of you want me to put pressure on the students to perform according to higher standards, while others think all learning should be fun. But I don't really think we'll get very far if we pursue either one of these lines of thought exclusively.

"I'm especially grateful for the contribution regarding the double challenge these youngsters are facing. Demanding top-notch performance during a period of active physical growth and development can bring about just the opposite of what we intend, but on the other hand we can't simply give in when we're confronted with the attitude of 'I don't want to; I can't; I don't feel like it today.' The bodies of preteens become heavy and are experienced as an obstacle for the first time. It's especially important for students of this age to learn to be independent and responsible, and responsibility always requires overcoming oneself to a certain extent. There's always some discomfort associated with that, and young people need to be aware of it and learn not to avoid it. It's unrealistic to think that anybody, even someone as young as our sixth-graders, can be happy nonstop from early in the morning to late at night. It's just not possible, and if we tried to make it possible, we'd be educating people to be unfit for real life.

"What's so difficult at this particular age, especially with such a large class, is to be fully aware of each student's personal situation. Not long ago one mother told me that her daughter had been absolutely unbearable until she got her first period, but after that she was a pleasant and easygoing person again. That adds to the difficulty of demanding better performance of the students, since each one is at a slightly different stage.

"Although we might wish for more enthusiasm and get-up-and-go on their part—we might want to encourage the idealism that awakens at this age—it is so difficult to actually achieve these high ideals.

"The issue is further complicated by the fact that the physical maturation process has accelerated so much that it all occurs in a very brief time span. Children today are missing out on a preadolescent stage of adjustment because they're maturing earlier; in a sense, they have to go through two developmental phases at once.

"But all this is not intended as a complaint—on the contrary. I've been working together with another teacher who has a lot of experience behind her—she actually wanted to be here tonight but couldn't make it due to health reasons. She's helped me find new ways to approach teaching this age group, and I have already had some very positive experiences I want to share with you this evening."

"Excuse me for interrupting, but before you do that, I'm concerned that we'll get a chance to talk about the shoplifting incidents while we're all here together," said one of the mothers. "Can you tell us how you see these thefts in context?"

"I asked the youngsters why they did it, and except for the ones who were simply going along for the ride, their motives all had something to do with the excitement of taking the risk—they wanted to find out whether they'd get caught or not, and whether they could outwit the grown-ups. I think each time they did it, it gave them a certain kind of pleasure and self-confidence. They had the feeling that they were grown up enough to ignore the authorities. You might recall the parable of good and evil that was mentioned at the beginning of our meeting—the parable of good and evil—the haughty ax can cut down the tree, but the tree points out that the ax's handle comes from the oak's trunk. What's called evil in the parable comes about by being separated from the good. Separation is what confronts us in the shoplifting incidents, too. To add a few of my own thoughts to the parable, if you think of the tree as having fruit and seeds, those are things that also separate out from the whole, but they carry the totality within themselves. It's not the kind of separation that leads to destruction, but the kind that leads to progress.

"We meet both of these aspects in this particular age group. Once they become sexually mature, the possibility to reproduce is there, but at the same time forces are freed up that allow individuals to take a separate stance in relationship to society as a whole. This yearning for independence can express itself in many different ways before the youngsters actually achieve real independence." Suzanne paused.

"Are you trying to suggest that even stealing is part of this developmental phase?" asked one of the fathers in a hostile tone.

Suzanne was still considering how to respond when Kelly's mother stepped in for her. "Absolutely. It's a factor in the development of humanity as a whole, not only of our children. Just look at the Old Testament story of the Fall and the expulsion from Paradise."

"It's simply a fact that we human beings cut ourselves off from the good at some point in time. Just look at what we have done to our earth, our water, and our air—let alone to ourselves. Our kids can see all that," said Heather's father emphatically.

Suzanne continued, "The new bridge that connects us to the world around us is built of insight and understanding, and that's the bridge these children are looking for now although it takes a long time to get there. When imitation was still what connected them with their environment, the connection was very direct and intimate, and even when they began to use their feelings to relate to their surroundings the connection was much closer than it is now. What we're trying to do now is help them build a new bridge out of thinking and the development of independent judgment. And progress with regard to environmental issues is also very slow, even though the people who have to deal with them are adults. Ultimately, people can develop inner freedom only through insight; they'll never acquire it as long as they are merely imitative or perceptive beings. Understanding is our only way of progressing from error to truth, and in that sense these shoplifting incidents may mean something for the children and help them get to know themselves better than they would have without going through that process."

"Doesn't that mean we mustn't condemn them as people, even though we condemn what they did?" asked Paul's father. "In spite of everything that's happened, we still have to recognize in them the good and innocent beings you described at the beginning of the evening."

"That can be pretty difficult sometimes; but you're right, that's what we have to be able to do," agreed one of the mothers. "A couple of weeks ago, Amanda came home after a crafts class absolutely fuming. She never liked crafts anyway, but this time she was really fed up. 'At the end of class I always have to dunk my bowl in water, and that makes it get all rough again so I have to start sanding from scratch and get it smooth again. And today that stupid teacher made me get it wet again. It just doesn't make sense—now it's going to get rough all over again, and I'm going to have to sand it one more time!' I suggested that she ask the crafts teacher why she always had to wet the bowl one more time. She did, and came home and explained to me that the wood swells up when it gets wet, raising the grain so that all the little irregularities come to the surface. If the bowl only gets sanded once instead of over and over again, it will slowly change as time goes on and get all rough and funny-looking.

"Aside from the fact that I was glad she felt some respect for the crafts teacher again after this explanation, I thought it was a wonderful image of what's going on with children of that age. They're like unfinished pieces of wood themselves, that keep getting dunked and having to be resanded. What's inside the piece of wood is brought to the surface, and then we can work on it. Actually, we ought to be grateful for every opportunity of getting these irregularities to come to the surface so they can be sanded smooth. If they all stayed inside, it would be disastrous for people's later development. We just have to be in agreement among ourselves, and then any one of us, whether in school or at home, will be able to exert a healing influence."

There was a brief pause in the conversation. Then one of the other mothers asked, "You said just a while ago that working with a more experienced teacher had helped you find new ways to approach the children, and that you were already experiencing positive results. I'd like to hear about what you did in class. Won't you tell us about that now?"

Suzanne was glad to oblige. "If we look at how the youngsters walk, we notice that it's a bit more uncertain than it was even a year ago, but there are also times when we can observe—if only briefly, for a couple of steps—that they're more likely now to put their whole foot on the ground. Birds can't do that, and neither can hoofed animals or beasts of prey; they all stand on their toes or only touch the ground with their claws. There's a time in the life of children, too, when they tend to walk on tiptoe. But now they're more and more likely to put their feet flat on the ground. The outcome of this period of relative awkwardness will be not only a new ability to take a stance and take a stand with their feet firmly on the ground, but also a new possibility for independence and individual points of view. Then it becomes something positive, a step forward. Concurrent with this change in how they walk, which is accompanied by a change in their use of gesture, I find whole new instructional possibilities opening up. Let me tell you one example.

"As you know, there are two boys named Bob in the class. I asked Bob to come to the board, and the one in question, who knew I had been looking at him, looked over at the other Bob, and gestured to him to go up to the board. Bob number two came up to the front and Bob number one relaxed in his seat; his little trick with the gesture had worked. What is that an expression of? It shows that they've discovered that gestures are actually language, a means of communication. When people grasp that gestures are language, drama becomes accessible to them, and each day I've been pleased to discover that the class is getting better and better at performing little dramatic dialogues. The children are pleased to be mastering a new area in speaking, and the dramatic speaking works back on their gestures and gait, giving them self-confidence in how they present themselves.

"Or your example from just a while ago, Mrs. DiPaulo: 'You're always *yakking*!' and Lori's response, 'I'm not *always* yakking." The only difference lies in the emphasis, and yet the meaning changes completely. Emphasis belongs to the will, but the fact that the sentence acquires a new meaning is a matter of thinking. Your daughter is trying to master both of them, and the physical basis for that is breathing. A few years ago, her breathing patterns would have been determined by imitation to a great extent, but now, because she wants to supply a different emphasis, how she breathes has to be totally different from how you breathe. She's determining how she breathes herself, controlling her breathing to express her own will and her own thoughts. That's another cause for rejoicing, because it means she's established her own point of view. But it goes without saying that once children have become able to express their own point of view through how they speak, they can use this very persuasively to convey things that are totally subjective."

"Yes, and that includes lying and turning things inside out so they're not true any more," burst out Alice Kovac's mother. "Now I understand that whole business with clean-up duty. Alice pretended to be *so* upset that she always had to stay after and clean up, and meanwhile she was spending that time pocketing stuff in department stores. What a nerve; I mean *really*!" A wave of amusement went round the classroom, and some of the parents suggested that it served her right for not asking to get Suzanne's side of the story.

"It used to be easier for us all to understand each other in class," Suzanne continued, "because everybody spoke more or less the same language. But now each of the children is struggling to discover a personal way of speaking and expressing what's on his or her mind. To begin with, it doesn't turn out quite right, and in exchange for them achieving individual vantage points, personal points of view, we have to put up with rudeness, disobedience, or lying. Still, we mustn't overlook what's actually trying to be born.

"Soon we're going to start practicing a dramatic scene to perform, and if the children have to play conspirators or drunkards or any other roles, the important thing is that they don't simply stay their ordinary selves and pretend to be someone else, but that they really grasp what their characters are like from the inside. They need a secure vantage point in order to do that, but it has to be found within the role of the conspirator or whatever other part they're playing. In effect, they have to put on a different character. The way they speak, which is now incarnating so forcefully into their gestures and their limbs—in fact, into their whole body—becomes a means of recognizing and portraying another person's essential character.

"It has also become apparent that there's a significant difference in the way boys and girls think at this stage. Let me give you an example. Two of the boys in the class came to me and wanted to know how to draw one or more tangents to a circle from some point outside it—through construction, not simply by eye. That's actually much too difficult for them still, but they were very insistent, and since we'd already done Thales' circle, I gave in. It was remarkable how the class was divided as we debated how to go about it—most of the boys showed an unusual interest in what was going on up at the board, while most of the girls were less involved. I even heard one of the girls say, 'I can't do it; I don't get it at all.' Meanwhile, the boys were volunteering all kinds of suggestions as to how to do the construction: 'Draw another line, a straight one; no, not like that—*there*; now draw a circle over there. . . .' And lo and behold, that group of boys—there was one girl among them, I'll admit— did discover how to carry out the construction, and I drew it on the board with a compass and ruler, according to their instructions. But now that the finished construction was there on the board, all of a sudden the girls looked up and got interested! I asked the class to see if they could do the construction on their own, and erased the board. Then an amazing thing happened. The first children to show me complete and correct drawings were girls—several of them. I looked over the boys' shoulders as they were working, and most of them were on the wrong track. They stopped, consulted among themselves, started over again, and eventually finished their drawings with some help from the girls.

"A geometric problem like this one has two distinct aspects—the drawing, which is the pictorial aspect, and the deliberations you have to go through in order to arrive at the right construction. This second aspect is not pictorial; it involves a deliberate inward process that can't happen as long as you're staring at the drawing. Boys often have more aptitude for this kind of deliberation than girls. They develop their 'ego will' in wrestling with the problem. Girls, on the other hand, tend to be more involved in their perceptions than in their will. That's what makes them say 'I can't; I don't get it' when it comes to so-called abstract thinking, which is a nonpictorial process.

"What can we learn from all this, then? We can see that taking a new step in thinking happens at the expense of our ability to visualize things. This sheds some light on what you were saying before, Mrs. Warner, about your son who's so good at thinking but can't find a key that's under his very nose and leaves his room in a total mess.

That's an example of someone who has lost his pictorial awareness. That hasn't happened with Lori, who can't do the problems and turns to her dad for help. She can't think without images yet. Usually, girls like that like to have one corner of their room arranged just so, with posters and photos and stuffed animals—all pictorial things. Of course, we don't want to encourage the children to be sloppy or to not try to do their math homework. But it means something different to us if we can see it in context, and the fact that boys and girls work and study together in school means that they can help make up for each other's shortcomings.

"We all need to develop the ability to think in abstractions. If we didn't, images would exert a magical control over us later on in our lives, paralyzing our independent judgment—we'd all still be afraid of the devil with his fork and horns, just as little children are. I suspect that all the criticism and moaning and groaning we're hearing from the children now is just a sign that their old pictorial consciousness is crumbling away so that something new, namely the possibility of independent judgment, can come about.

"And why are old friendships falling apart and new ones being formed? One of you mentioned little groups and rival cliques that compete with each other. The old sense of community we used to have in the class isn't there any more, and it's often both surprising and puzzling to me to see which students are drawn to each other, and how strongly.

"I'd like to give an example from the curriculum to show you what direction this development is taking. This year, we will be discussing the decline of the Roman Empire and the concurrent rise of Christianity as a new element in world history. We'll be learning about a man named Benedict of Nursia, who studied Roman law as a young man and then saw how the Vandals invaded Rome, murdering and plundering as they sacked the city. There was no one who could make them have any respect for the law; nothing was left of the law except some dead letters on a page. Benedict dropped his studies and moved to Mount Casinus with a small group of men who called each other brothers. There he founded the first monastery. Instead of living according to external laws, they all made an inner commitment to lead their lives according to the rules of the order in their search for the Christ, the Lord of destiny. In the course of the sixth grade, this subject block may help us overcome much of what has disrupted our togetherness in this transition phase, and perhaps a new sense of community will come about on a higher level.

"I hope these epigrammatic remarks have helped you see that there's a deeper meaning to the profound difficulties the class is going through. Let's not permit ourselves to be swayed by the one-sided picture the momentary situation presents, at least not without inquiring into its real meaning. Of course, bad and even tragic things can and will still happen—at this age, boys and girls simply want to break out and run away. And where are they running? Toward themselves, toward what they want to be deep down inside, but what that is can only be permeated with light and warmth once everything, literally everything, has been individualized. To describe the result of this process, Rudolf Steiner coined the phrase 'earthly maturity,' which encompasses many more aspects of development than the more commonly used, one-sided term 'sexual maturity.' The artist Emil Nolde experienced something of this earthly maturity when he was fourteen. He describes how he was roaming over the fields by himself, driven by thoughts and feelings that weren't exactly clear to him. In a field where the grain was tall and no one could see him, he lay down on the ground on his back with his eyes shut and his arms stretched out. As he lay there, he thought about the Savior as he was being taken down from the cross. Then a vague but powerful feeling of joy made him turn over and hug the whole big round wonderful world. He wanted to embrace the Earth like a lover."

After that, the parents' meeting slowly broke up. Here and there, the conversation continued for a while in small groups. Many people expressed a desire for an ongoing opportunity to work together, and Suzanne promised them a study of puberty from a holistic point of view.

She was full of mixed emotions on the way home. Kathy was waiting for her in great expectation. "How was it? How did it go?"

It was late, but Suzanne was glad to sit down and have a cup of tea. "Well, if I'd done it six months ago, I would have considered it a full success, but after everything that's been going on with the class, I felt a bit like I was either explaining or apologizing all the time."

"But would you really have been able to do it six months ago?" prodded Kathy.

"Of course not. I didn't have the experience I have now, and Harriet has really helped me a lot in the meantime."

They chatted for a long time. "But you know," said Suzanne as she finally got up to go to bed, "I forgot to tell you my most important discovery of the evening."

"What's that?"

"I realized for the first time how important it is to be *real* with the children, to be open and unpretentious. Until now I always thought that the lesson had to go just the way I'd planned and the kids had to respond in a certain way. But that's not how things are in real life. You have to count on the unexpected happening, or not count on anything and simply be open to whatever new thing is going to strike you next."

"Well, on that note, I guess we'd better say good night. See you in the morning!"

SUGGESTED READING:

Hermann Koepke, *Encountering the Self: Transformation and Destiny in the Ninth Year*, Anthroposophic Press, 1990.

Rudolf Steiner, *The Spiritual Guidance of Man*, Anthroposophic Press, 1970.

PART TWO

Individual Stories

| 7 |

Homevisits

The first half of this book has given us an overview of Suzanne's class as a whole and has attempted to portray changes in attitude common to preteens in general as well as the range of reactions they arouse in their parents and teachers. In order to discuss in greater depth several of the more serious difficulties children of this age may encounter, the next two chapters tell the individual stories of two of the students in the class.

Many parents confronted with the question of what kind of education would be best for their child believe that choosing the appropriate school is enough to guarantee that their son's or daughter's development will proceed harmoniously. On the other hand, it is not at all uncommon for teachers to be of the opinion that all the difficulties of a problem child can be traced to the home; in that case, they believe, there is nothing they as teachers can do to foster the child's progress. This is a very common vicious circle and it is rare that either side manages to break it. The first section of Chapter Seven will use the example of Gordon, a student in Suzanne's class, to help us examine this subject more closely.

People directly involved in the education and upbringing of children often think that only what children really experience through seeing, hearing, doing, and understanding can be of any help to them. But is that really true? Is it really only our actions that tell children what we are like, but not our concealed thoughts and feelings? The second section of Chapter Seven, which recounts the story of Kimberley and her mother Joan, will give you an opportunity to resolve this question for yourself.

1 / Conversations with Gordon's Parents

Gordon always liked to stay in bed as long as possible. Finally, when he heard his mother calling for the second time, he reluctantly got up and pulled on the usual baggy pair of pants. He ate little for breakfast, scarcely bothering to chew. He liked toast only if it was really sweet, so he ladled on the jam until it ran over the edge. On mornings when he didn't have time to eat, his mother put two pieces together so he could at least eat a sandwich on the way to school.

Late as he was, however, Gordon still took the time to rush into the bathroom. He squirted hair-cream onto the palm of one hand, then rubbed his hands together and ran them through his hair. He checked in the mirror to make sure the cream was getting stiff, combed his hair straight up, and secured it with hair spray. Then, satisfied with his handiwork, he made a quick search of the apartment for his tapes, notebooks, and other school paraphernalia, and dashed out the door.

His mother went into his room. "Same old mess," she commented, shaking her head. The air was stuffy. She went to the window, opened it wide, and turned back the covers to air the bed.

Some of Gordon's classmates got on the bus at the stop after his. One of them had his hair sticking straight up, just like Gordon's. In fact, Gordon had copied it from him. The two of them looked like a pair of porcupines.

"Good morning, Gordon," said Suzanne, grasping his hand firmly. He couldn't think of anything more unpleasant than this greeting, because she wouldn't let go of his hand until he had looked her straight in the eye. Then he had to show her his homework—make-up work, assignments he hadn't had ready for yesterday. He rummaged around for a long time, and finally pulled out a dog-eared notebook. He knew what was coming. He still hadn't done the most important part, and what he had done was sloppy. He gave a little nod as if in agreement, but actually what he hoped to achieve was some hint of good will on his teacher's part. So he nodded again and promised to be all caught up "by tomorrow." Suzanne wrote down the missing assignments in his notebook and asked if he had understood what he was supposed to do. "Sure, sure," said Gordon, and finally he was allowed to go to his seat.

Gordon felt quite at ease as he sang and recited and played the recorder with the rest of the class. He was just looking up at the ceiling thinking about that motor he was going to rebuild, when. . . "Gordon!" Oh, no, the teacher had called on him. She repeated the question, and at the same time someone prompted him from behind: "The cowboys!" "The cowboys," he stammered, and the whole class roared with laughter. Gordon laughed too, hiding his uncertainty under the mask of the class clown and pretending he'd pulled off a real good one again. When recess time came, he looked up and saw one of his classmates standing beside him, a girl he particularly liked.

"The cowboys weren't the original inhabitants of America," she said, laughing. For the first time Gordon realized what the question had been.

English class began with writing from dictation—a pretty hopeless undertaking as far as Gordon was concerned, but the boy sitting next to him turned his notebook in Gordon's direction. At first Gordon made a big effort to keep his eyes on the teacher, but eventually he broke down and squinted over at his neighbor. The next class was math. Gordon could still follow what was going on as long as they were doing fractions, but when it came to algebraic equations, he gave up and copied from someone else.

By the end of their two-hour gym class, Gordon was dripping from the effort. His team had won, but he had lots of ideas about how they could do even better next time. He was quite red in the face as he exhorted his teammates. He got so carried away that no one else could get a word in edgewise, so soon they stopped listening to him.

"No homework today; we finished it in class," he said when his mother asked. But then he recalled what he had promised that morning. He sat down at his desk with good intentions, but his glance fell on the comics he always swapped with his classmates. He started to leaf through them, but then he noticed that the tape he'd taken to school was missing. Where could it have gone to? He got out his walkman. The next thing he knew his father was home and it was time for supper.

After supper, Gordon told his mother that he had to "go get something" and left quickly, shutting the door behind him so fast she didn't have time to ask any questions. He went straight to where he thought that girl he was enamored of would be, and sure enough he found her there.

She had seen him, too—in fact, she looked right at him. Gordon pulled out a partly smoked cigarette and lit it as he strolled past. He quickly took a few puffs, and then remembered the cowboys, and wondered what she had thought about that.

When he went home, he managed to sneak up to his room so quietly that no one heard him. The main thing was to avoid any questions about what he'd gone to get. He sat down at the desk without making a sound. There was his homework notebook. He skimmed through Suzanne's instructions and wrote a couple of sentences without putting much thought into them. "Can that be right?" he wondered. Who could he ask? Oh, well, too late now. Maybe on the way to school tomorrow he'd bump into somebody who could tell him what to do. He chewed his nails for a bit and then went to bed, leaving his clothes flung over the chair. His baggy pants had fallen to the floor.

"Gordon, where are those assignments?" He was standing in front of his class teacher. "I don't know . . . I couldn't . . . we got out of school so late yesterday."

"*Gordon!*" Suzanne said his name again with all possible emphasis.

Gordon nodded in agreement. He'd agree to anything if she'd only let him go sit down. At least his handwriting was nice, she commented sarcastically; the lower loops were so long that one line obliterated the next one down. He nodded again. "Tomorrow's your last chance, Gordon!"

"Ok, tomorrow!" Yes, he promised. Yes, he understood what he had to do. Finally he was allowed to go to his seat.

"Gordon, where are your assignments?" It was his teacher's insistent voice again. The same old story all over again, for the third morning in a row. "I don't know ... we had so much to do ... no, not yesterday ... I, I...."

He saw his teacher's disappointed face. He really did feel sorry; he really did want to do better. As usual, Suzanne was jotting something in her class diary, and this time Gordon was especially uncomfortable standing there watching her write. He must have been a funny sight in the eyes of his classmates—a scrawny figure with a pale face, eyes glued to the floor, baggy pants slipping down. And on top of it all, his hair stuck up in spikes like the comb on a rooster. Suzanne finished writing and told him that she was going to have to speak with his parents. Gordon went to his seat, casting a glance in the direction of the girl he liked and was relieved to see that she was involved in a lively conversation with some friends. Probably she hadn't been watching at all while he was standing up there at the teacher's desk.

Suzanne was itching to find a way to get through to that boy. She was really worried that he was learning so little. And each time she spoke with him, she was struck by how poor his articulation was. In spite of years of speech exercises and recitation, he avoided using consonants almost entirely; on the other hand, whenever the class got rowdy, he was always the loudest.

Suzanne's colleagues had also been complaining about Gordon—especially the foreign-language teachers. It was impossible to get him to talk, and his reading was just a stutter. His dictations were full of mistakes and his vocabulary was absolutely minimal; he had a memory like a sieve.

In vain Suzanne looked for something that Gordon was good at, something worthy of recognition. But in the course of her ponderings, one streak in Gordon's character caught her attention. It was the melancholy attitude he put on, although he was actually sanguine in temperament. Somewhere he must want to be part of the class and be recognized for what he does. . . .

Suzanne had been thinking about visiting his parents for some time. She called them up, and was surprised to learn that Gordon's mother was no happier about her son's behavior than Suzanne herself. It was practically impossible for her to say anything to him any more, she said. All he did was hole up in his room and listen to tapes. But what concerned her the most was the fact that he was smoking so much. Suzanne made an appointment for a home visit, and one evening not long afterward she was standing at the door of their apartment.

Gordon's father folded up his newspaper and offered Suzanne a seat, while his wife went upstairs to make sure the younger children were asleep. Mr. Molnick asked Suzanne what she would like to drink and passed her request on to his wife. Then he lit up a cigarette and settled down to hear the sad tale of how Gordon was doing in school. "I know things aren't going well with him. At home, I'm the only one he listens to; my wife can't really get through to him any more. But I wonder if it's not just a phase he's going through, a necessary change like the ones you talked about in the parents' meeting."

Suzanne hesitated. Answering that question in the affirmative was not going to change the basic problem. Gordon was already thirteen; he was the oldest one in the class, and his behavior was not at all typical of the class as a whole. "Of course puberty is part of the problem, but we have to realize that Gordon has gotten so out of balance that he isn't going to be able to straighten himself out on his own. In my opinion, he's really at risk."

That answer didn't sit well with Gordon's father, and Mrs. Molnick looked at her husband with a worried expression on her face. "I don't know what to do about it, either," she said. "I mean, we chose this special school for him and everything, and in spite of it all, he's still blowing it, and *you*"—with a reproachful glance at Suzanne—"don't seem to know how to handle him, either."

"We've got to know exactly what we have to do," said Mr. Molnick emphatically. "The only problem is, my wife and I both work. Her job's just part time, but neither of us is around to sit on the kid all the time."

"Why do you think Gordon's in such rough shape?" Suzanne interjected.

"We don't know; that's what we're all sitting here for. That's what we want to find out from you. What are we supposed to do about it?"

"Do you have a good relationship with your son?" inquired Suzanne, turning to his father first.

"Of course I have a relationship to him, I'm the only one he listens to—well, not always. What do you mean by relationship, anyway? It used to be better, but now he doesn't want to have anything to do with me. He doesn't ask me anything; he doesn't come to me with his problems—except when he needs money, which is pretty often."

"Does he trust you? Do the two of you have a conversation once in a while?" Suzanne probed further.

"You say something about that," said Mr. Molnick, turning to his wife, who was looking very unhappy. "Like I said, he doesn't want to have anything to do with me."

"I don't think you could really call it a conversation when we talk. As soon as he comes home, he gets something to eat and then goes to his room. About all he says is, 'Come on, Mom, where is it?' There's an outburst if he can't find something, and recently he's taken to helping himself to anything and everything—including my husband's cigarettes—without bothering to ask."

"Do you think his smoking is such a bad thing?" asked Mr. Molnick. "I mean, other boys of that age smoke, don't they? I've smoked only moderately ever since we were married, and my wife smokes too, though not nearly as much as I do."

Suzanne thought he was putting the cart before the horse, so she said, "I think Gordon's smoking is just a symptom of something else. It surely isn't the reason why he's stuck in a rut now."

"Well, what is the reason, then?" It was obvious that Gordon's father was challenging Suzanne with that question.

"What do *you* think it is?" Suzanne asked, turning to Gordon's mother. Mrs. Molnick shook her head. "I really don't know. All I know is that Gordon's impossible to get along with at the moment. I don't know what to do about it. No matter what I say, he just withdraws. Like my husband said, the only time he approaches either of us is when there's something he wants."

Both parents were silent. So was Suzanne. Smoking, tapes, class clown—they all seemed like attempts to escape from reality. It was as if Gordon were waiting for someone to come looking for him.

Gordon's mother was the first to break the silence. "Do *you* have a relationship to our son?" she asked Suzanne. Suzanne knew she couldn't pretend to be doing any better than they were. "I'm trying hard, but I can't say that I have," she replied.

"Does he have any friends in the class?" asked his father, looking for a clue. Suzanne had to respond in the negative. "He's generally well liked, but he doesn't have any particularly close friends. How does he get along with his little brother and sister?"

"When the other kids were really little, he always wanted to play with them, which was a help to me since I had to work as well as be a housewife," his mother replied. "He tried to help in other ways, too, but when he put the dishes away, for instance, everything ended up in the wrong place. I could do it quicker and better myself, and often he just got in the way. He doesn't help at all any more. Let Mom do the work, that's what she's there for! And he's so spaced out."

"He wasn't always that bad," commented Mr. Molnick, "at least not when I gave him a swift smack." "But that didn't do any good!" his wife interrupted. "Not any more, but it used to," insisted her husband, "though I will admit that he's really starting to bear a grudge against me if I let my hand slip now and then."

Gordon's parents went on talking about how things used to be, interrupting each other frequently. Suzanne got a vivid impression of what life at home was like for Gordon. She imagined how it had been when his mother came home from work and nothing had been done in the house, and then his father came home. . . . Probably Gordon, standing around doing nothing, had been a ready scapegoat for the two of them.

Suzanne saw that there was nothing more she could hope to accomplish that evening. She wanted to talk it all over with Harriet and get her advice. She suggested that to Gordon's parents, who seemed not at all impressed with the idea—maybe even somewhat disappointed. They had nothing better to suggest, however, so they did not object.

"It's important for you to check Gordon's homework," said Suzanne, "and I'll write the instructions in his notebook so you can see what he's supposed to do. But that won't be enough. I'm going to try to think of other things that might help Gordon, and then we should get together again."

Gordon's father had obviously been turning something over in his mind, but he checked himself and said nothing. It wasn't hard for Suzanne to guess that he wasn't too pleased with the school.

The next day, Suzanne called Harriet and asked if they could get together to discuss Gordon and his difficulties. Harriet made Suzanne tell her about both the parent-teacher meeting and her visit with Gordon's parents in great detail, interrupting with a question every time Suzanne tried to shortcut by simply giving her own interpretation of what had happened. "Please tell me *exactly* what happened," she insisted, and Suzanne had to oblige.

When they had finally gone through everything, Suzanne waited expectantly for what her colleague would say. Harriet, however, did not respond immediately, but sat thinking for a while. It was a long time before she spoke.

"Gordon's situation and the difficulties he's going through sound very familiar—typical of people that age," she said, to Suzanne's great surprise. It reminded her of Gordon's father's reaction to what she had said about Gordon in school. But although her words were similar, they had a different ring to them.

Harriet reached for a pencil and paper, but put them down again. "Gordon is taking every possible way out," she said. "He's avoiding everything; he'd just as soon be invisible. 'Escape' is his motto; he can't establish a connection to anything. And the reactions he's getting at home and in school—no offense intended—just make matters worse. On the other hand, he's at the mercy of all his many wants and desires and has found very sophisticated ways of satisfying them. Between those two extremes, there's actually nothing left of the real Gordon except a little bundle of misery. That's why we have to help him.

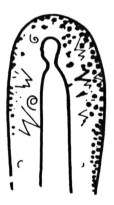

"Do you remember the sketch you made a couple weeks ago? I'd like to refer back to that and take it one step further." Harriet outlined two human figures. Around the first figure, she drew a little dome and filled it in with all kinds of doodles. Then she filled in the second figure with everything that had been outside in the dome around the first one. "Sketches and diagrams are always just a crutch," she cautioned, "and we can't go on using them for too long, but I think this will help you see what I mean. Gordon's father hits him when he does something wrong, and so instead of relating to what he was supposed to do, the boy's will is alienated from it. His mother prefers to get the work done fast and doesn't let him help because he does a bad job, so he gets the impression that he can't do anything right and resigns himself to being a good-for-nothing. All this emotion and will that wasn't accepted used to be out here, around and outside of him—that's why I drew them in the little dome. But after age twelve, young people don't just live in this cloud of stuff all around them; they experience its content inside themselves. Everything that has accumulated outside him has turned into Gordon's inward experience. If at this point he has no will to work and can't relate to anything, it's because of what he experienced earlier. It's like having it reflected in a mirror, only there's a time lag—what we're seeing now is what used to be all around him."

"But isn't it too late to do any good, then?"

"Never! It may be late, but it's never too late to help!" Harriet's eyes were flashing, and Suzanne was taken by surprise. Suddenly the older woman sitting bolt upright in front of her reminded her more of a freedom fighter than a retired teacher.

"It makes no sense, though, to demand something of the boy when he doesn't have it in him. After all, we wouldn't expect flowers we hadn't planted to grow in a garden, to use a very simple example. The children in your class have gone through different developmental stages that are interrelated in the same way that growth, flowering, and bearing fruit are dependent on each other, and there's a good reason why you as a class teacher accompany the children in your class through all that. It could easily happen that the next gardener would have only a vague idea of what her predecessor had planted, not to mention the fact that it wouldn't have been growing in her all this time, too. And it might also be that a new teacher would have no idea of what had been going on at home and wouldn't be able to take it into account in the right way."

"Doesn't that mean I'll have to do some catching up with Gordon to strengthen his will and his feelings so he'll be able to learn?" asked Suzanne.

"Right," said Harriet, "and how will you go about doing that?" She looked at Suzanne expectantly.

Suzanne, however, wanted to take advantage of the older woman's rich fund of experience, so she kept quiet about her own views on the subject and returned the question. "What would *you* do in this situation, Harriet?"

Harriet was ready with a concrete example. She positioned her pencil carefully on the top of the desk and then said with quiet determination, "I'm putting this pencil down here on the desk. The point is toward me and the eraser is pointing toward the wall. The sides of the pencil are orange, and the desk is light brown. The pencil and the corner of the desk form a right-angled triangle with two sides approximately equal in length." She paused for a second. "And what does that have to do with Gordon? What do you think an action like that, coupled with a visual impression and a spoken sentence beginning with 'I', would mean to him?"

"He could do it, of course," said Suzanne, thoroughly confused. "Nothing could be easier, but I'm sure he'd wonder what for. It would probably seem pointless to him, or even silly.

"All right, but then you tell him that he can improve his memory with little exercises like that, so he'll be able to remember where he put the pencil next time he needs it. And you're right that doing something like that is pointless. It would be much more to the point if you would invariably put the pencil back in your pencil box, so you wouldn't have to remember where you'd put it. In itself, this activity has absolutely no purpose; the value lies in its effect. It is an activity that doesn't satisfy any particular desire or longing; if you do it at all, you do it out of absolute freedom. Nothing outside of you is limiting or determining what you do in any way. You're the one who chooses the object and the place to put it, and you're the one who experiences the visual impression of it. That free space is exactly what Gordon is lacking and has to learn to create for himself. Practically nothing he does comes from an independent center; it all comes out of an ego that's either distracted by and enmeshed in wants and desires, or thrown back on itself in the experience of 'I can't do it.'"

Suzanne was doubtful. "I can't imagine how that can possibly be enough to help."

"Well, you said nothing could be easier than this exercise. But I've done it with my classes, and I can assure you that even I found it very difficult in the long run to keep on doing it and other similar exercises. I found out that you really have to force yourself to keep on doing something that 'pointless.' You really have to confront yourself very strongly. After that, you can go on to the other exercises Rudolf Steiner suggested. They're all in the public lecture called *Overcoming Nervousness*; you really ought to study it carefully. Whenever I was teaching youngsters of that age, I always got it out and studied it again, and then we practiced some variations on the exercises in class. They may seem simple, but they're very effective if you keep doing them long enough."

Harriet saw that Suzanne was still skeptical, and added, "To begin with, of course, I wasn't at all convinced there would be any positive result. But that was just prejudice on my part, and it disappeared all by itself as we went on practicing. I'm sure the results will convince you, too, but you need all the patience and love of a gardener while you're doing it. I'll be eager to hear about your experiences." Fully aware of the impression she was making on her young colleague, Harriet scanned the desk corner with the pencil again, as if checking to see if the arrangement conformed to her memory of its colors, forms, and angles, before picking up the pencil as deftly as if she were playing pick-up-sticks. Suzanne had never seen anyone so completely involved in what she was doing.

"One more thing," said Harriet, "It's very important how you act toward Gordon. For instance, if he's standing in front of the class and hasn't done his homework again, you can be generous and say, 'Good morning, Gordon. I'm not checking any assignments today, but how about surprising me with your notebook tomorrow?' Don't say it ironically, though; he has to be able to hear the humor in your voice. Lighten up, and lighten him up too! Any smile you coax out of him is worth a thousand times more than the profound shame he's bogged down in at the moment. That's how you need to approach him as long as he's in such bad shape. Later on, when he's gotten himself together a bit, you can be more demanding again. After all, there's no way we can go through life without ever experiencing shame, and it does provoke new insight."

"Do you think I should suggest these exercises to his parents, too?" asked Suzanne tentatively.

"Do one or two of them with your class first, and make a note of how your students respond—Gordon in particular, of course. Whatever your experience with Gordon is from now on should be the basis of your next visit with his parents. Don't try to tackle the shortcomings in Gordon's home life directly— that would be the wrong way to approach things, and it could make his parents feel guilty or unleash their aggressions, which wouldn't be good for Gordon. It wouldn't make your position any easier, either. We've learned a lot about Gordon's background that helps us understand him better, and we would be able to do the same with his parents if their biographies and upbringing were as accessible to us. It may not be easy to accept a child's home and family for what they are, but it's the best way to go— unless, of course, the situation is really extreme. That's an exception.

"One thing you do need to address directly, though, is the negative effect of rock music. There are a lot of tapes that extol sex, violence, and undisguised Satanism. Sometimes the texts are recorded backward—that's called 'backward masking'— so that their content is only taken in subconsciously. In subliminal recordings, speech vibrations are transformed into musical vibrations so that we're not consciously aware of what we're actually hearing. There's an awful lot of sexuality, brutality, and Satanism on video, too.

"While we're on the subject, I have to tell you about an experience I'll never forget. I was involved in a conversation group at one point, and there was one man in the group whose expression really struck me. It was as if his big eyes were radiating goodness and light, but crying at the same time. In one session we were talking about drugs, and finally he spoke. He had always been able to talk about anything at all with his son, he said, and they had been very close. But one day he noticed that he couldn't get through to the boy anymore; their intimate connection was gone, wiped out. In retrospect he realized that around that same time his son had gotten into the habit of falling asleep listening to his walkman, so that even in sleep he was being flooded with rock music. I'll never forget the expression on that man's face when he added, 'And then my son got swallowed up by drugs.' I was sitting very close to him, or I wouldn't have been able to hear what came out as a mere whisper, 'All I can do now is pray.'

Suzanne recalled her dream about her students on the skating floor, and felt as if she were standing in front of an abyss. "Reacting with fear or outrage, understandable as that might be, is not going to help us accomplish what we have to do," said Harriet gently, and Suzanne looked up at her. "And there's one sure way to improve class spirit. If you start looking for the real Gordon and trying to help, the whole class will rejoice with you when the lost sheep is found."

It was as if Suzanne had undergone a transformation during that conversation with Harriet. She had caught something of Harriet's fiery enthusiasm, and it inspired her to prepare the next day's main lesson in a totally new way. It was as if she had found a mission, but it had nothing to do with the Gordon with spiky hair and baggy pants, with the boy who was constantly getting distracted and stood there in front of her every morning with his homework still not done. No, she was no longer bound to that image. She had looked too deeply into his character for that, had heard his cry for help and let it resound within her. Nothing was going to harm that boy; nothing could harm him now that she had joined forces with him. She was looking forward to the next day at school, to meeting Gordon again, to the time when this strong new impulse would start to work.

"Good morning, Gordon!" Her voice was clear and happy, and she was smiling. "Good morning, Miss Kulp." It was the first time he had ever said her name. For a second he stood there as if rooted to the spot, then hurried to his seat.

Suzanne introduced the "misplacing" exercise first thing, even before morning verse. One of the girls, responding to suggestions from the class, spread a newspaper out on the floor at the back of the room and put a stack of notebooks on it. "I'm placing the stack of notebooks on the newspaper," she said. "The notebooks are green, and the one on top has a red mark on it. The newspaper is sticking out all around the notebooks." She couldn't think of how to go on, and one of her classmates prompted, "The notebooks are rectangular, and the stack forms a right angle with the newspaper."

"Very good!" Suzanne praised them. She was glad to see that Gordon had been totally with it. As they began the lesson, the mood in the classroom was unusual, and Suzanne could tell that all the youngsters were alert and with it. When the main lesson was over, many of them gave Suzanne the sign they had agreed upon—right index fingers concealed in the fingers of their left fist—as a signal that it was time to put the notebooks and newspaper back where they belonged.

Having made sure that the whole class understood the exercise, Suzanne asked them to take turns deciding what to "misplace," and where to put it. When Gordon's turn came, he fished a cigarette lighter out of his pocket and came up and put it on her desk. "It's black, rectangular, and has a green spot on it, and I'm putting it on the desk." Suzanne looked at it more closely; the green spot was actually a trapezoid. Gordon quickly turned the lighter around, grinned, and said in all deliberateness, "That spot on it is a green *triangle*." He and Suzanne both laughed, and Gordon went back to his seat.

Suzanne had always made a practice of recalling the main lesson at the end of each day and reflecting on how it had gone, and this time she paid particular attention to Gordon's behavior. The next morning, she was all prepared to skip checking his homework, as Harriet suggested, but when Gordon came in he was carrying his pack of books under one arm and waving his notebook under her nose with the other. He was radiant. Suzanne accepted the notebook—still full of dog ears—as if it were a birthday gift.

She also started experimenting with something else after the "misplacing" exercise—each morning they spent a short time practicing letters in a calligraphic script. The shape of the letters was different from what they were used to, so the students had to pay extra attention to how they were writing, and Suzanne encouraged them to draw each letter with care. After a few days, when she could tell that Gordon was also getting into it, she called his parents and scheduled another visit.

Gordon's father had the evening paper in his hand when he opened the door for her, and he said that he was still waiting for his wife. He sat down again and went back to reading the paper. Suzanne could sense what was going on in him. She remembered all too clearly what frame of mind he had been in at the end of their last visit. Clearly, he was still disappointed both in the school and in Gordon's performance, and he was making no attempt to conceal his displeasure. To Suzanne he suddenly seemed just like Gordon, cut off from what was going on around him and feeling no connection to anything. It was another little revelation. But she was still rejoicing at the thought of how Gordon had greeted her the other morning, and of how he had come in today waving that notebook, without her even asking for it. She was full of the image of the other Gordon—not the way he looked now, but the way he could be—and it came bubbling out of her. "Mr. Molnick, your son handed in his assignments without even being asked. They were done right, and even the handwriting was neat. I was so pleased with him! He's really pulled himself together."

Whether it was the good news from Suzanne or the fact that his wife had just come in, Mr. Molnick came out from behind his newspaper. He put it aside, amazed at this young teacher's cheerful response to his boorishness. He looked as if there were something on his mind he wanted to say, but his wife beat him to it.

"At least he's been listening to us again, ever since I smashed his walkman and threw it out," she burst out, before even acknowledging Suzanne's presence. "I should have thought of that much sooner. You always told us what a bad thing it was for kids to drown themselves in that kind of music, Miss Kulp. But now he's really working. He's sitting upstairs doing his homework. At this time of night, he'd usually just be listening to his tapes."

Suzanne bit her tongue so as not to blurt out, "That's not what I'd be doing if you had smashed my walkman." Fortunately she had enough presence of mind to realize that Gordon's mother was extremely agitated. And she had at least been trying to help her son. Now was not the time to try to make her understand that this was a case of the ends not justifying the means. Suzanne restrained herself, making a mental note to be on the lookout for an opportunity to say something appropriate about walkmans and rock music later on when all these emotions had subsided a bit.

"Huh," Gordon's father muttered, not at all convinced. "He'll just go right back to listening to them when he's talked me out of enough money to get a new walkman."

"Oh no, he won't," said Mrs. Molnick triumphantly, "because I threw out all his cassettes too. And if you go on giving him money for stuff like that, it's your own fault. But he's been a totally different boy ever since then. Go see for yourself. He's sitting upstairs practicing calligraphy."

"What are you teaching them that for?" asked Mr. Molnick. "Gordon's penmanship is lousy—scarcely legible, in fact, so why are you having him practice this fancy stuff?"

"The letters of this calligraphic script are fairly similar to the script Gordon has already learned to write, but enough details are different so that he really has to pay very close attention to what he's doing in order to get it right," Suzanne explained. "That means he has to get very involved in what he's doing, and that's the whole point. Eventually it will help him calm down and become a more balanced person."

"I'll admit he's quieter, but I bet it's because he doesn't have that music going all the time any more," Mrs. Molnick claimed.

"Both things are probably helping," agreed Suzanne. She could see that her answer hadn't satisfied Gordon's father, however.

"People are supposed to learn things in school that they'll be able to use later on in life," he insisted. "I want my son to learn how to do things so he'll be able to manage on his own. He may be getting a kick out of practicing calligraphy now, but what good is it going to do him later on? I think he ought to be learning to write legibly in ordinary script, and practicing his spelling and arithmetic, and learning other things he'll really be able to use. The way it is now, he's wasting his time in school."

Suzanne could see his point of view. After all, he was only putting into words something she herself had been guilty of for far too long in trying to teach Gordon. She, too, had only wanted to get something out of him without ever considering the prerequisites, let alone helping him to master them. "Last time I was here, one of the things we talked about was how Gordon's lack of motivation was preventing him from learning because he had trouble paying attention in class and getting his assignments done. To put it briefly, he couldn't get sufficiently involved in what he was supposed to be doing. And that's exactly what he's practicing now, to develop his character. Being able to pay attention will help him in all his subjects, but he has to get a handle on it in some unrelated area first. That's why we've been practicing calligraphy."

"But you could do the same thing with arithmetic," objected his father.

Suzanne agreed, but went on to try to explain to him why a seemingly pointless activity would work better in this case than an activity taken up for its utility value rather than for its own sake. "Whenever your independent character, your ego, is not swayed by the purpose or advantage of doing something, you create a space you can live and breathe in—that is, if you also don't just let yourself fall into indifference, which is what shows in a page of sloppy ordinary handwriting. If Gordon can manage to love what he's doing, to take a real interest in it, then his work will strengthen him. It has just occurred to me, though, that if you'd rather do something similar with numbers, you could try giving your son a number and asking him to tell you what it would be in reverse—27 becomes 72, 301 turns into 103, 528 turns into 825, and so on. The point is for him to force himself to be really with it in order to visualize how it will turn out." Gordon's father seemed content with that.

"You seem to know about a whole lot of interesting exercises," Mrs. Molnick commented. "Is there one for learning how not to be a slob? That's what Gordon really needs."

"I have a booklet by Rudolf Steiner that's full of helpful exercises," replied Suzanne, "and I'd be glad to lend it to you. He doesn't address the problem of sloppiness directly, but there are several exercises that have to do with it. For instance, there's an exercise for becoming aware of how you habitually do things. It's not so easy to get a picture of how you sit or walk or eat, but it becomes somewhat easier if you can see the consequences of your usual way of doing things, as you can if you look at something you've written. You and Gordon could do that together. If you've been writing on unlined paper, does your handwriting always go straight across the page, or are some of the lines at a slant? Are the letters nice to look at, or not? The most helpful thing for Gordon would be to experience how nicely his page of writing has turned out. Looking back over what you've done is what awakens the kind of strength we want to encourage. For example, you could also ask him to recall what his room looks like. Has he put things away? Has he put any pictures or posters on the wall?—that kind of thing. What kind of an impression do you get of his room the way it is now?

"Awful, just awful, that's how his room looks," groaned his mother.

"We can take that as a reflection of what he's done," said Suzanne, "an externalized image of his intentions and deliberate actions. And by learning to get his room in order, he'll learn to get his own will in order, too."

"You're absolutely right; his room needs cleaning out and tidying up from top to bottom. You wouldn't believe how many times I've told him that, but he still can't do it by himself!" Mrs. Molnick complained.

"Once in a while you get so fed up you do it for him, don't you?" Suzanne guessed. "Try doing it with him instead. It has to reflect *his* intentions, *his* will, not yours. If you clean up after him, his room only reflects how *you* want it to be. But since he can't do it by himself yet, he needs some support from an adult. I know it's a big temptation to do it yourself because you can get it done faster and do a better job, but it's not the outward difference that matters here, it's what can change inside Gordon. It'll help Gordon much more if he learns to keep his surroundings in order by himself, and you simply support him in the process. If you can look at it from that point of view, sloppiness is an excellent opportunity for a little ego exercise on his part."

"Did I understand what you said at the parents' meeting about boys' sloppiness being either a result or a prerequisite—I forget which—for their new kind of thinking, which is relatively abstract and image-free in comparison to how girls go about it?" asked Gordon's father. "Doesn't that mean we have to put up with a certain amount of sloppiness from boys that age?"

Suzanne answered, "When I referred to untidiness in the parents' meeting, I meant that we can see it as an expression of how the youngsters' thought processes are changing. I was trying to show that the new capacity for abstract thinking they're acquiring often goes hand in hand with a certain amount of sloppiness, particularly among boys. That was the point I wanted to illustrate when I described how differently boys and girls approached the task of doing a geometric construction. The girls had the advantage over the boys when it came to actually doing the drawing, and the boys definitely have something to learn from them about how to come to grips with their visual impressions. Mastering their visual impressions helps people develop self-control, and being a slob is simply a manifestation of lack of self-control. So it's extremely important for boys to learn to be accountable for the state of their surroundings and possessions—in other words, to clean up their mess. If they've tidied up around them, it works back on their ability to control themselves in other ways, such as not having to give in to their wishes if that's not appropriate to the situation."

"Talk about wishes—Gordon seems to be nothing but a great big bundle of them at the moment! 'Wishes' is putting it mildly, actually; 'irresistible urges' would be more like it. His smoking, for instance. Aren't his classmates egging him on to do it?" asked Mr. Molnick. "Whenever I tell him not to smoke, he just does it anyway, but behind my back."

Suzanne hesitated, unsure of quite how to respond. On the one hand, she didn't want to infringe on Mr. Molnick's freedom of choice; on the other hand, a lot could be gained by being absolutely straightforward if she could pull it off right. Gordon's father noticed her hesitation, and took the bull by the horns himself. "Of course, the two of us smoke too, and he can't help seeing it. And even if we tell him that he is still growing and that he should wait until he's grown up, we are not setting him a very good example. That's probably a big reason for it, right?"

Suzanne, visibly relieved that Mr. Molnick could be so open about it, nodded in agreement. "One of the exercises in the pamphlet I mentioned is to make a practice of denying yourself some little wish now and then—something that's only a matter of comfort or pleasure and that doesn't do any harm if you have to go without. It's very helpful in developing self-control."

"I'm sure it is," agreed Gordon's father, "and it's fine if I do that for myself. But if I try to make him do it, it only makes him smoke more, and besides, he just thinks I'm an old man and life is passing me by, don't you see?"

"Well, let me go back to your own example," answered Suzanne. "If your son sees that you're smoking less, that would make an impression on him. And if you don't try to forbid him to smoke, but forbid *yourself* and make sure that he notices what you're doing. Even without saying anything to him directly, it can make a very big impression."

"I don't know if you ever smoked yourself, but whenever I tell myself I don't want to smoke anymore, even if I make a resolution and write it down, my thoughts come right back to smoking again, and I can't stop thinking about it." Mr. Molnick laughed, ruefully. "It's enough to drive you nuts!"

"I smoked, too, when I was in college," Suzanne admitted. "I only quit when I started teaching and realized I didn't have the energy for both teaching and smoking. What you tried to do, by the way, reminds me of Kant when he had to dismiss a servant he was very fond of, because the man had been stealing from him. He couldn't stop feeling sorry about it, so he put up a sign on his wall saying, 'My servant must be forgotten.' Of course it didn't work. We have to take the quirks of human nature into account."

"Yeah, I guess that's what it boils down to," laughed Gordon's father. "But what's the method? There must be a trick to it."

"It isn't easy," replied Suzanne. "Making a resolution means you have to be able to get free of yourself. That's what happens anyway when there's something you hold as an ideal—it's like walking toward a light that will be there lighting your way forever. But if you want to repress something, it's like trying to hold a ball underwater. As soon as you let go of it, it bobs to the surface again."

"And what do you do to make it stay down?"

"I don't think you can—trying to repress something is the wrong approach. You have to think of something that seems even better to you than having a cigarette, and when you're struck by the urge to smoke, you fill yourself with that thought until it outshines the urge to smoke. Your ideal might be how much better the air is to breathe when it isn't all full of smoke, or maybe how your physical stamina will improve if you quit. Whatever it is, it has to be something compelling, something that really means a lot to you, or it won't work."

"You know, for Gordon's sake . . . that would be an ideal worth working for, to give it up for his sake so he'll grow up healthy!" Gordon's mother broke in enthusiastically.

"Maybe you can do that," objected her husband, "You don't smoke all that much anyway. But I'm looking forward to it all day long at work. I'm in quality control, and. . ."

"Yes, but just think how much you could look forward to a happier, healthier Gordon!"

Mr. Molnick gave in. "Oh, well, let's try it. It certainly wouldn't hurt, even if I only manage to cut back while my wife quits altogether." The Molnicks both laughed.

"If you're really serious about it, though," Suzanne cautioned, "don't try to quit all at once. What I did was figure out how much I was smoking per day, on the average, and then tried to smoke one cigarette less every day. And in the meantime I was trying to experience my ideal more and more vividly."

The tension in the air had receded markedly during this last part of the conversation. All three were more relaxed now, and it was much easier to talk. Suzanne told the Molnicks about school and how she was trying to inspire ideals in her students. Gordon's mother mentioned the peculiar way her son walked—just like an actor he'd seen in the movies. His ideals were idols, in most cases.

"It's important for them to be able to choose their heroes for themselves," commented Suzanne. "I often find that my own heroes and heroines simply don't speak to what's going on in the children. But it would be good if you could make a point of talking, perhaps at supper time, about a lot of different people who had high ideals they fought hard for—people we don't study in school. I can't get terribly excited about the hundredths of a second that make a difference in athletic competitions these days, but if your son idolizes one particular athlete, for instance, you can point out how that person's disciplined effort to master his own body can serve as an example for Gordon. Those people can't afford a single drop of alcohol or one puff on a cigarette."

"Do you mean to say that whatever idols they choose, we'll always be able to find something good about them?" asked Gordon's mother doubtfully.

"Why not!" replied Suzanne spontaneously. "It's important for us to always see both sides, both the pros and the cons. How else are children going to learn to judge for themselves and come to the right decision? Otherwise, we're just foisting off our own opinions on the youngsters, who usually reject them, although we ourselves see no need to question their validity. . . ."

"Darn right we don't," said Gordon's father smugly. "But the problem with that is that Gordon knows right away what he wants to do. He doesn't allow any time for pros and cons."

"That's certainly one side of the question," Suzanne agreed. "But on the other hand, he also starts a lot of things he doesn't get around to finishing because his motivation runs out on him. But weighing up the pros and cons can strengthen our motivation and our resolve. We saw an astounding example of that in what happened on a recent eighth grade class trip. The two sections of grade eight both went to the same cabin in the mountains, one after the other, and both classes decided they wanted to see the sun rise from the top of the mountain. In one class, every single student, even the less sturdy ones, came along and made it to the top, even though it was a good two-hour climb. Only part of the other class made it. It turned out that the teacher whose whole class made it to the top had seriously questioned whether or not they ought to attempt that hike, and he had asked the boys and girls to think of as many pros and cons as possible. Then he asked them to think it over again until the next day and only come to a final decision the next morning. The decision was unanimous, and they never faltered in their resolve to reach the top."

"It does give a lot of weight to your decision if you've been that thorough about it," commented Mrs. Molnick.

"Everybody feels they've had a say in what you're going to do. We could try that too, some time."

"I'd like to suggest that you try weighing the pros and cons like this in a conversation about rock-music tapes," said Suzanne. "Gordon's just at the age when his own insight needs to start replacing authoritative measures that may well seem arbitrary to him. I'll leave you a couple of articles about rock to get you started. If he understands something of what's at stake, Gordon will be more likely to accept the loss of his walkman, and what your husband was afraid of—that Gordon would get another one as soon as he gets the chance—is less likely to happen."

"Seems to me we ought to give it another chance and not take Gordon out of the Waldorf School right away. What do you think?" Mr. Molnick asked Suzanne.

She had half expected it, but it still came as a shock. "Did you *really* want to take him out of the school?"

"Well, we thought he might do better if he were made to toe the line more strictly, but it might well be that he'd just give up totally instead. That's why I think we ought to wait and see whether he's reached a peak or whether he goes on improving," replied Gordon's father.

Suzanne realized that now a lot depended on what kind of a relationship she could establish with Gordon's parents. If they were simply going to take the attitude of "Let's wait and see" and not intervene positively in their son's life, then Gordon was still at risk. She would have to arrange another visit as soon as possible and encourage them to take an active role in their son's education.

It was late when Suzanne finally left. She thought about Gordon's father most of the way home. Hadn't he been about to say something at the beginning of her visit, only his wife beat him to it? Suzanne was almost certain what he would have said, and it seemed to her as if some higher power had miraculously intervened in their conversation and made it possible for Mr. Molnick to change his mind in the course of the evening. Thinking back on it, she was a bit scared to remember that she'd been making all kinds of suggestions that didn't come from her own experience, but were simply things she had read about. Luckily for her, Gordon's father hadn't seemed to mind.

Gordon's mother had been very supportive, though, and her outlook on her son had changed totally. Suzanne had to think of Harriet, who had made it possible for her to find a connection to Gordon. Actually, everyone in the circle of people concerned about Gordon had something to give, some inner effort, something to overcome.

Something else occurred to Suzanne that she wanted to bring up with Gordon's parents. Perhaps Gordon could take karate lessons. Then he'd learn about leverage, points of rotation, and centers of gravity via his own body. It would give him some practical experience in physics that would fit right in with next year's curriculum, when the class would be studying mechanics and the laws governing leverage and falling bodies. Besides, he would be among people who had absolutely no use for nicotine or alcohol. Suzanne made up her mind to find out if there was a karate club that would be right for Gordon.

Maybe she should have a word with his mother about what she was cooking, too, since Gordon's frequent difficulty in concentrating might also have something to do with one-sided eating habits. It would be good to find out whether he was eating too much meat and not enough salads or grains, or whether he overdid it on sweets. That was another topic for her next visit with the Molnicks.

But why had Gordon's situation become so acute?

Suzanne slowed her pace, thinking that he might well have gotten into such a rut because the adults involved in his education and upbringing had had too little opportunity to share their thoughts. As she walked on, it became clearer and clearer to her that raising and educating children is a work adults undertake in common. "There's no way it can work if the grown-ups in question don't want to have anything to do with each other," she thought. The total lack of connectedness that Gordon seemed to be suffering from only reflected the fact that the adults in his life hadn't taken enough sincere interest in each other.

SUGGESTED READING:

Cookery Book, Lucas Clinic, Rudolf Steiner Press, 1989.

Martin Large, Who's Bringing Them Up? Television and Child Development: How To Break the T.V. Habit, 2nd ed., Hawthorn Press, 1990.

Sheryl and Mel London, Creative Cooking with Grains and Pasta, Rodale Press, 1982.

Jerry Mander, Four Arguments for the Elimination of Television, Morrow, 1978.

Neil Postman, Amusing Ourselves to Death: Public Discourse in the Age of Show Business, Penguin, 1986.

Carl A. Raschke, Painted Black: From Drug Killings to Heavy Metal, Harper-Row, 1990.

Betty Staley, Between Form and Freedom: A Practical Guide to the Teenage Years, Hawthorn Press, 1988.

Rudolf Steiner, Overcoming Nervousness, Anthroposophic Press, 1969.

2 / Visits with Kimberley's Mother

In first grade, Kimberley had been one of the most willing and hardworking children in the class. She would count to a thousand for any grown-up who had the patience to hear her out and could perform all four arithmetical operations using two-digit numbers. In second grade she could already spell most words correctly, and her main-lesson books were exemplary. But after second grade, Kimberley had to leave the class; her mother, recently divorced, no longer wanted to live in the same town, and moving meant changing schools. Kimberley's leaving was painful for all concerned—for herself, for the class, and for her teacher. So everyone was glad when, three years later, they moved back into town and Kimberley rejoined her old class. She had changed quite a bit in the interim—she was a lot taller, her hair was cut short, and she had become very assertive. She knew exactly what she liked and didn't like, and showed it. There no longer seemed to be any danger of her becoming a teacher's pet.

After sitting in on Suzanne's main lesson, Harriet had made Suzanne aware of possible changes in temperament in that age group. She had put it more or less like this: "With the onset of earthly maturity, we often notice a change in temperament, a change that's already been prepared during the last transition phase around age nine. Some children keep the same temperament, but as a general rule, if they do change, cholerics become sanguine; sanguines, phlegmatic; phlegmatics, melancholic; and melancholics, choleric. You'll need to pay particular attention to the melancholic girls because all girls, in contrast to boys, develop a strong relationship to their circulation as they mature. That means all girls, regardless of temperament, acquire an extra choleric streak at this stage, and it expresses itself as stubbornness or opposition. So any girl who was melancholic to begin with and then switches temperaments becomes doubly choleric. These two factors coming together are more than enough to turn a docile young melancholic into a raging, willful, and spiteful choleric. It comes as a great surprise, and the girl's parents usually aren't prepared for it at all. If you don't watch out, girls like that can go completely overboard."

Since Kimberley had been melancholic as a little girl, Suzanne had made a point of keeping her in mind with regard to what Harriet had said. She did notice a certain amount of willfulness appearing, but it was more melancholic than choleric, and was certainly no stronger or more pronounced in Kim than in any of the other girls, so Suzanne dismissed the possibility of a real change of temperament in Kimberley's case. And during grade 6, Kimberley changed in a way that seemed to totally contradict Harriet's statements. Her occasional willfulness and the undercurrent of defiant independence suddenly disappeared. Instead, Suzanne saw a girl with a casual flair who arrived in class relaxed and cheerful. All of a sudden, her accomplishments in artistic subjects were outstanding for someone her age, and she won first prize in a city-wide artistic competition.

But after a few weeks, this phase passed. It became more and more common for Kimberley to be late for class. She didn't complete her homework and looked tired and sleepy, often sitting with her elbows on the desk, supporting her head in her hands. The old flair was gone, and she wasn't just tired—she was sad. Suzanne could find no explanation for what was going on. Even the way Kim dressed was different—she was choosing black clothes that contrasted markedly with her pale, tired little face. Was the old melancholic putting in an appearance again, stronger than ever? During recess, Kimberley often hung around alone, while in class she had trouble concentrating. She still had moments of liveliness now and then, but on the whole her work was deteriorating rapidly. This strange change worried Suzanne. When she spoke to Kim's subject teachers, they said they had also observed these symptoms in her and had no idea what to make of them. It was decided to schedule an in-depth conference on Kim with the school doctor and all her teachers.

The next day, Kimberley was absent. The day after that, she brought in a note from her mother explaining her absence, but a few days later she was absent again, this time with no excuse. Soon she missed school again, and this time she tried all kinds of excuses and got all tangled up in them. Suzanne could tell that the girl was losing the ground under her feet.

Getting hold of Kimberley's mother was difficult. During the day she was always at work, and in the evenings no one answered the phone, but finally Suzanne did catch up with her. The woman sounded distraught and unwilling to talk over the phone. She agreed to meet with Suzanne and promptly hung up.

Suzanne felt uneasy as she rang the bell at their apartment and waited, hearing the footsteps inside. Kimberley's mother opened the door, making an attempt to conceal her tear-stained face as she let Suzanne in. The two women sat across from each other in silence for a moment before Kim's mother broke the oppressive stillness and confronted Suzanne with the news that Kimberley had been smoking hashish, mixing it into cigarettes she rolled herself. A lump of hash that her mother had found under her mattress was right there on the table.

Suzanne was speechless. How could she possibly have watched this develop and not understand what was going on? In fact, the brief phase of accomplishment, which Suzanne had been so pleased to see, had signaled the beginning of Kim's drug use. Then had come the exhaustion, the isolation, the lies and illusions. Kimberley's conference had been scheduled, but it was too late to prevent what had already happened.

That evening, Suzanne got a clear picture of what Kimberley's life was like at home. Right after the divorce, she and her mother had been very close, but when they had moved back into town, her mother had started dating one man steadily, and his intrusion into their comfortable intimacy provoked a fiery protest on Kimberley's part. The girl declared her independence in a way that was totally unexpected of someone formerly so docile. She slammed the doors, refused to eat with her mother and her boyfriend, and even went so far as to smash the dishes against the wall. In school, she carefully covered up her choleric temperament, but at home it broke out in full fury. Eventually, the tension between Kim and her mother became so great that Kim stopped coming home after school. Once she even stayed out all night.

Kim's mother was overcome with self-reproach. She was sure Kimberley had turned to drugs in protest against her mother's new partner. "Unfortunately," she said bitterly, "this man can't relate to my daughter at all. I can see that fate has handed me a very difficult decision to make—I'm going to have to choose between my daughter and Dan. No matter what I do, I stand to lose someone I love dearly." Suzanne tried to get her to take heart, but she refused to be comforted. "I don't see any sense in living if it's just going to go on like this," she sobbed.

They sat together for a long time. More often than not they were silent, but Suzanne did learn a lot about the other woman's difficult life. Eventually Kim's mother said she felt better and thanked Suzanne for her patience, but as soon as she thought about her daughter, the tears started streaming down her face again.

Suzanne recalled the time she had gone to visit a colleague who was terminally ill. On his deathbed, he had quoted something from the Greek, and it had made an indelible impression on Suzanne. She thought of him and dared to use the same words, "If there is anything greater than the fate decreed by the gods, it is the human being who bears it without faltering."

"For my daughter's sake...," Kimberley's mother couldn't get any farther than that. Finally she stood up, thanked Suzanne, and saw her to the door.

Her last words had given Suzanne grounds for hope. If Kimberley lost the one person who was fighting for her, she would only get deeper into drugs. Suzanne's task, she perceived, was simply to help Kim's mother chart her course through troubled waters on something other than purely emotional grounds. She needed to consider carefully what she was going to do. For Kim's sake, something decisive had to happen very soon.

Kimberley came back to school the day after next, bringing Suzanne a letter from her mother. "Dear Miss Kulp," the letter read,

I didn't sleep at all the night after your visit, but spent the whole time struggling with the choice between Dan and Kimberley. At first I decided to put Kimberley in a group home, thinking that the change and a well-ordered life would help her make a fresh start. It didn't seem right to me to try to go back to our little family of two. But when I imagined Kim in a home, no matter how good a one it might be, I realized that was a pretty flimsy solution, especially because I knew it was going to be absolutely crucial for Kim to have someone to confide in. So before I went to work that morning, I decided that I was going to be around and available for my daughter again—not in the same old way, but as a helper, friend, and partner who'll stick by her through thick and thin. I'm glad I came to this decision, and if Dan can't accept it, well . . . Kim and I belong together, and if the three of us can't work it out, then Dan will have to do without me too. Kimberley still hadn't come home when I left for work, and I didn't see her until I got back that evening. I can't tell you what all came out in the conversation we had, but Kim is very concerned about the possibility of being expelled from school. She really wants to stay in your class, and she's vowed not to take drugs anymore. Thank you for all your help, and I hope you'll be able to come and talk with me, or rather with both of us, sometime soon.

Sincerely yours,
Joan Gilmartin

Suzanne reported all this in an emergency meeting of the teachers. The faculty agreed that Kimberley would not be expelled, providing she live up to certain very strict conditions, and the suggestion was made to form a special committee to follow up Kimberley's case. Harriet was sitting on the edge of her chair as they discussed the issue. "I surely don't want to block this suggestion," she interrupted, "but I do want to make sure we keep one crucial point in mind. We have all heard enough of Kimberley's biography to realize that she has already been through one great shake-up at a very early age when her mother's first marriage ended in divorce. That wound was able to heal only because of the strength of her mother's love. Joan devoted herself exclusively to her daughter in the period right after the divorce. But what happened when another man entered her life? That's what provoked all the difficulties we're facing now. I think Joan's willingness to risk this new relationship for the sake of her commitment to her daughter shows that she's capable of an admirable objectivity about her own very sensitive situation, and I hope and pray that she will be able one way or another to devote sufficient energy to turning her daughter's life around. After all, thoughts, feelings, and attitudes are real forces in our lives and are just as potent as our visible actions. On the other hand, I don't think we should even hope that this decision of Joan's will bring about a permanent solution. Joan has a right to her adult life and relationships, and it wouldn't be healthy for either of them in the long run if Kimberley were allowed to totally dominate her mother's life. They're going to need a lot of help to work this out—everything we can give and professional counseling as well."

The next evening, Suzanne stood in front of Ms. Gilmartin's door again. Kimberley let her in. Suzanne asked her for a full account of her drug use and insisted that she confess to all the lies and excuses she had used to try to conceal it. After she had told the whole truth, Suzanne told her the consequences the faculty had agreed upon. She would have to live up to the conditions very conscientiously, or she would not be allowed to remain in the Waldorf school. She was not to go out of the house unaccompanied and was not to be absent from school without excuse. If in spite of her sincere resolve to give up drugs totally, she were ever to backslide, she was to admit the incident to either her mother or her teacher immediately. She was to get her homework done on time without exception. These conditions would be subject to review after six months, and the proposed committee would meet with Kimberley, her mother, and Suzanne every two weeks to check on how Kim was doing.

Kimberley had two relapses in the next nine months. The first time, she admitted the incident to her mother right away; the second time, she was caught smoking. On both occasions, lengthy conversations followed. For Suzanne, however, the deciding factors were Kim's renewed willingness to work, her availability in class, and the acceptance and support of her classmates. Suzanne kept her eye on Kimberley and did everything within her means to make sure that she would be able to stay in the school.

Six months later, Suzanne bumped into Joan downtown one day. "There's something I've been meaning to tell you about for a long time, Suzanne, but I have been hesitant to talk about it in front of the whole committee. That first time you came to visit, Kimberley didn't come home all night. She still hadn't come back when I left for work, but she was there when I got home in the evening, collapsed in a miserable little heap there in the kitchen. There was nothing left of her old defiance. We started to talk, tentatively at first, and then she said, 'Mom, I want to tell you this dream I had.' I couldn't wait to hear it. She had dreamed about being down in a cellar that was like a deep pit; there was no way out. She said I had looked down at her once and then disappeared. It was a long, long time before I came back and let down a rope so she could climb out. That was what she had dreamed that night when I was struggling with having to make a choice between Kimberley and Dan."

SUGGESTED READING:

Arta Rehabilitation Center, Rock Bottom: Beyond Drug Addiction, Hawthorn Press, 1987.

Rudolf Steiner, The Four Temperaments, Anthroposophic Press, 1988.

Rudolf Treichler, Soulways: The Developing Soul-Life Phases, Thresholds and Biography, Hawthorn Press, 1989.

| *8* |

Progress Reports

Rudolf Steiner expressed the wish that each Waldorf student be given a yearly progress report that was primarily intended to be inspirational in character, although it should also point out what the student needed to work on.

This final chapter contains a series of reports written for one and the same girl. They are reproduced here with her permission, but her name has been changed. Using these reports, we can study the turning points that occur around the ages of nine and twelve in the course of a child's development and see how some things change while others seem to persist stubbornly.

The class teacher's report is complemented by those of the subject teachers. The number of subject reports increases over the years—there are only two or three in second grade, but by sixth grade there may be as many as nine. More and more observations by more and more teachers are compiled, and the way the child is addressed changes accordingly. In the early grades, the children recognize themselves in the images of the stories in their reports; later on, their subject reports give an ever clearer reflection of their performance. These subject reports have not been reproduced here. I want to emphasize this especially, because otherwise it would be easy to get the impression that these written reports only convey a vague image of the student's accomplishments and that specific subject-oriented assessment does not take place.

THE DEVELOPMENT OF ONE GIRL
AS REFLECTED IN HER PROGRESS REPORTS

Sandra was a charming little girl with a long, thick, black braid, a narrow little face and laughing black eyes. Everything that went on in her little world was whispered into her teacher's ear: Witches went flying through the air at night; her dolls came alive at Christmas; maybe her rabbits would be able to talk, then, too! Sandra was a live-wire, full of laughs, giggles, and surprises. Her delicate little fingers deftly turned tiny lumps of clay into cats, birds, or snakes. She was also very light on her feet and always had little dances to perform. She was especially good in painting, drawing, writing, and reading. But there was one big stumbling block for her—arithmetic. She really hated it, hated it so much that she stayed home sick whenever the class had arithmetic. And there was one other thing that was difficult for her. In spite of being full of ideas and very communicative, she could only whisper these things in her teacher's ear. If she had to speak from her seat, it came out so quietly that almost no one could understand it. She was a sensitive child and was anxious, or maybe only shy, when there were lots of other children around. At home, she spent a lot of time alone with her mother, who said that at home Sandra spoke in a normal tone of voice, often laughing loudly and even pestering her mother. How could this girl who was so shy but so very imaginative be encouraged to come out of her shell and contribute some of her precious energy to the rest of the class? That was the main question her second-grade report was meant to address. Like the others in the class, Sandra had received a picture and a verse at the end of first grade.

Any direct approach to the problem, anything outside the realm of images, would have been totally foreign to this little girl. "You have to involve the child's imagination," Rudolf Steiner had once said to a teacher in a similar case. Taking that into consideration, Sandra's second-grade report had to be embedded in a story so that Sandra could enjoy this image of herself and yet feel gently challenged.

SECOND-GRADE REPORT FOR SANDRA

Dear Sandra,

Once upon a time there was a little white mouse who was very pretty. She wore a little silver crown between her ears and had rosy pink paws. It was a pleasure to watch her dancing in the mouse-palace where she lived. On long winter nights when the moon was shining into the mouse hole, she brought out her little fiddle and played fine silvery music on it. A big fat beetle bug followed the sound of the delicate tones and flew in right over the little mouse's head, making such a terrible droning noise that she was scared practically out of her wits and dropped the fiddle. Another time, the little mouse was sleeping under a big golden flower when a buzzing bee flew up. The mouse trembled all over—she was so frightened and her little mousy teeth chattered so hard she couldn't keep her little mousy mouth closed anymore. And once when she was walking beside a brook, a fish jumped out of the water and scared her so much she almost fainted. And you can just imagine what it was like for her when a big bird flew right over her head and twittered at her from a twig. But that was just too much for the little snowy-white mouse. She got raging mad and whistled through her teeth at the bird, a great big whistle that was so loud that the bird took off immediately.

"Who gave you such a strong voice?" asked an ant who had watched the whole thing in great astonishment. "God," said the little mouse without stopping to think. "God, who made all us animals. You and me, too." That was like a light going on for the mouse, and all of a sudden she realized she didn't have to be afraid. After that, when anybody tried to scare her, all she had to do was whistle at them.

Every evening the little mouse folded her rosy little mousy paws and prayed, praising God. She sang:

> The least of all the little beasts
> That live upon the earth
> Is not too small for Thee, dear God—
> 'Tis Thou who gave them birth.
> To Thee, both men and beasts sing praise
> And in their joy their voices raise.
> For Thee the bird sings,
> For Thee the fish springs;
> For Thee all the beetles and bees
> Buzz loudly in trying to please.
> To Thee the little mouse so white
> Gives praise each day and through each night.

CLEMENS BRENTANO

This story reminds me of what school has been like for you, dear Sandra. You can do so many things that only a special little mouse can do. You are very good at modeling, dancing, making animals, writing, and reading. You've even learned to do arithmetic a little bit, and often you paint very beautiful pictures. I don't know whether or not you can whistle through your teeth, but maybe you don't need to. A mouse can't make any sound except a whistle, but a person can talk. And if you will learn to speak loudly and clearly—in school, too, not just at home—then you will be able to do much more than the clever little mouse, who can only whistle.

Someone who can say what she wants in a loud strong voice needs to have courage to do that. But where does courage come from? For a long time the mouse didn't know, until it finally occurred to her that this courage comes from God, because without His help no one could do anything. And God, who helps even the smallest animals, will surely help you too. Just try it, and you'll find out how brave and strong you really are!

Your teacher,
Suzanne Kulp

According to her parents, Sandra had been very pleased with her report. However, she was much more interested in the mouse-palace and its pleasures and treasures than in following the mouse's example of loud, courageous speaking, and the role of the timid mouse still seemed tailor-made for her. During the transitional phase around age nine, all children go through some kind of crisis or turning point that brings them into themselves more strongly than before, and Sandra, too, underwent a profound transformation. The story of Creation made a very strong impression on her. When the Paradise Play was being performed, she sat there with big eyes taking in everything that was happening on stage, including how God the Father conjured up a human being from under a sack. A faint smile of profound understanding flickered across her face as she watched this scene. From that point on, Sandra was much more self-confident. She had cast off something belonging to her early childhood. Her lovely voice began to be heard—not always, though; only when the occasion warranted it. Her confidence in a higher power guiding her destiny still needed deepening and strengthening, and that's how her third-grade report came about.

THIRD-GRADE REPORT FOR SANDRA

Dear Sandra,

Once upon a time there was a beautiful little snow-white mouse. It was evening, and the mouse was getting ready to pray. I bet you think she folded her rosy little mousy paws and sat there bolt upright, supported on her tail, while she whispered something into her paws. But no, that's not what happened this time. Just imagine—there on the floor lay the mouse's pelt with the little tail, the rosy paws, the snow-white little mousy teeth and the two little round ears. The little silver crown rolled across the floor and made a few loops before it fell over. You see, when the white mouse was all ready to pray, suddenly her fur split open and fell on the floor at her feet, and there stood a human being who had been inside the mouse skin.

Dear Sandra, you may be surprised and wonder why that happened. But I think you actually know deep down inside what was happening, even if you have to think about it a bit. The little mouse threw off her skin, and a human being came out. That must seem familiar to you; you've seen something like it before, in the Paradise Play. You saw God the Father, and there in front of him was the first human being he created. But you couldn't see that person yet, because he was all covered with something brown. Then God the Father breathed into him His living breath—the human soul—and in that moment the brown covering fell to the ground, and there stood Adam, a human being. After that, Adam learned many things that the other creatures couldn't learn.

You, too, have learned a lot this year, dear Sandra. The stories from the Bible, in particular, were something you took in very deeply. You painted many lovely pictures on your own and gave them to me, to my great delight. Your writing is nice and neat, and you've even made a little progress in arithmetic. That will get even better in fourth grade; you'll see.

But let's get back to Adam. What did he learn next, after he had learned to stand upright? He saw all the glories of creation, and because he took them in so deeply, the living breath of God within him was transformed into speech—wonderful, strong, resounding speech. You too can speak in a strong and resounding voice when you want to, and you should always want to, dear Sandra.

When a person speaks to God in prayer, out of the fullness of her heart, her thoughts become full of light. You might also say that something falls away that would otherwise cover up the brightness of her thoughts. That's how someone becomes free, courageous, and happy, and how she learns to truly think. And as you get older, each year of your life speaks to you deep down inside. I wonder what those years will tell you?

This prayer by Rudolf Steiner will be a good guide for you.

Your teacher,
Suzanne Kulp

I look into starry realms—
I can understand their shining
When I can see in them
the wisdom of God's guidance of the world.
I look down in my heart—
I can understand its beating
When I can feel in it
the kindness of God's guidance of mankind.
I know nothing of the light of stars
And nothing of the beating of my heart
When I neither see nor feel God.
"God has led my soul
Into this earthly life;
And He will lead it ever on to new life,"
Say those who know right thinking.
And every year that we shall live
Will tell us more of God and of the soul's eternal life.

RUDOLF STEINER

After the third grade, Sandra took a major step in her development by stepping out of the world of her imagination (although that always remained vivid for her) and into her surroundings. This transformation was apparent right down into the way she walked, putting her feet on the ground much more resolutely and self-confidently than she could have done before. The pictures she drew were no longer purely the products of her imagination, but grasped what was characteristic of a rude and rowdy starling or an owl that sends shivers up your spine. She made more and more room in her heart for the world around her. On the whole, arithmetic was the only subject in which she made no breakthroughs. She wrote about her experiences in little compositions she used to leave on her teacher's desk before Suzanne arrived in the morning.

It was clear that until now the arts had served her well but that she needed to develop her potential to serve their cause. That is what her fourth-grade report was intended to express.

FOURTH-GRADE REPORT FOR SANDRA

Dear Sandra,
Geography, human and animal studies, and the Norse legends of gods and heroes caught your attention in the fourth grade and called forth a lot of beautiful work on your part. How you opened your eyes and looked around you when we studied local geography, and how interested you were all of a sudden in what had surrounded you all these years! And how well you worked when we studied animals—your starlings are real brats, your owl wings its way through the night like a ghost, and your parrots gossip their heads off in the jungle. I clearly remember these and all the other beautiful pictures you painted in the course of this block. You were involved with all your heart and soul.

When we practiced alliteration in the block on Norse mythology, you tried to stamp your feet hard on the floor to the beat of the poem and made a real effort to speak the alliterative sounds loudly and clearly. Like a force working within you, something broke out and resounded through the room.

I got to see much more of this inner strength in the many compositions and pictures you did of your own accord and gave to me. They showed me a whole world of sight and sound that was pouring out of you.

However, all these wonderful strengths need the firm ground of clear thinking under their feet, and that's something you can practice in arithmetic. You have a good grasp of calculating with fractions, but decimal fractions still elude you—unfortunately you were sick a good deal while the class was studying them. But you know how to think just fine, so why shouldn't you be able to do arithmetic just fine too?

As I look back over the last few years, I can see something that was nothing more than a mouse's whistle at first, changed into speech when the mouse's skin fell off and a human being stepped out of it. Language and speaking allow a person to create something like a brand new world, and this world comes about when you listen and set down in words what is burning inside you.

Your teacher,
Suzanne Kulp

The clouds are adrift and the stars run their courses,
The larks fly as high as the sun's golden horses;
Then, soaring in bliss to the heavenly gate,
They listen to words that the seraphs relate.
From heaven's expanses the lark then flies
    earthward
Remembering the things that her ears and her
    heart heard.

And tells them in clear ringing tones, like a bell,
To winds and to waters, to flowers in the dell.
Then breezes and blossoms and waves full of whispers
Pass it all on to their most trusted sisters,
And people who listen can hear what they've heard
And set down the heavenly song in words.

ROBERT HAMERLING

Sandra was now at the end of her childhood as such, on the very brink of preadolescence. At this age, a person's inner and outer world need to come into balance, but in Sandra's case the inner world was still stronger than the outer. The purpose of this report was to make her aware of this slight imbalance and to turn her great inner strengths a bit more toward the outer world.

FIFTH-GRADE REPORT FOR SANDRA

Dear Sandra,

We started off the fifth grade by studying trees. You spent a long time sitting reverently over your watercolor paintings until you managed to capture the essence of each tree on paper—the youthful light of the birches, the far-sighted pines on a slight rise, the oaks strong and fiery, the firs self-contained and thoughtful. In your heart of hearts, you were able to listen to the very being of the trees, and out of that you were able to paint these beautiful pictures. But you also looked at the trees out-side—the birch tree in the playground, the pines you love to stand under, and our old linden tree. When you stand under a tree for long enough, you can sense its strength, and then you can paint out of this strength later on. It is a very special strength, fully alive. It's what the trees live on, and people can pick up this strength and make use of it for their painting.

Each morning this year, we've spoken some words that relate to this:

The World-Creator moves
In sunlight and in soul-light,
In worldwide space without,
In soul-depths here within.

RUDOLF STEINER

We've only been speaking this verse since the beginning of fifth grade, because only now are you at the age when both the inner and the outer world contribute equally to how you stand in life.

In history this year, we learned about the ancient Indians and Persians. It was easy for you to relate to the Indians, who held the whole world in their souls. The Persians, though, were the first to take the step onto the Earth. They knew that it was up to human beings to decide whether the Earth could become the dwelling of the Sun spirit or whether it would be ruled by sinister Ahriman. They did not avoid the conflict, but cultivated the earth and combated the forces of evil, never giving in to them without a fight.

We also cultivated our eye for the external world by doing freehand geometric drawings. The last thing we drew was a chair, and at first it wasn't at all easy for you to draw that chair exactly as you saw it. You had to look at it more and more closely, and in the end you succeeded. That was brave of you, Sandra!

You had a similar experience with arithmetic. You were sick for a while when we were studying it, but not for as long as in other years. You're beginning to see the light.

Your compositions turned out exceptionally well again. You have a knack for capturing the essentials in just a few words. Your spelling is good, too, though not always perfect.

In sixth grade we will concern ourselves still more with the outer world when we sculpt wood, plant a garden, and do experiments in physics. But we will be able to do all this right only if we have the inner strength for it—the inner strength that also slumbers in everything outside us, where we may find it and awaken it.

Your teacher,
Suzanne Kulp

What a human being sees clearly in the outer world
Is only what [she] can illumine with [her] inner light.

RUDOLF STEINER

Sandra, like many of the girls in her class, did not experience the passage into earthly maturity without a certain amount of defiance and resistance. However, the revolution leading to a breakthrough into abstract thinking, which is always based on an attitude of faint resistance or antipathy, was kept in bounds in her case. She did go through very changeable phases, though. Her long thick black braid seemed to reach all the way down to her early childhood, while her alert gaze and more forceful speaking seemed to point to the future. She finally managed to take the long-awaited step forward in arithmetic. In view of the extreme changeability adolescents experience, Sandra's report for the sixth grade was an attempt to consolidate her gains by means of positivity. It was complemented by nine subject reports.

SIXTH-GRADE REPORT FOR SANDRA

Dear Sandra,

Sculpture and gardening, mineralogy and geometry, a different school building in a different location—you encountered many new things in this past year. And you, too, changed as the year went by. You have grown taller, your gaze is more awake and your speaking both somewhat stronger and richer with all the dramatic nuances of resistance and negation.

Your consciousness is beginning to be transformed, right down to the very depths of your being. Solid land masses are appearing within the old pictorial stream of consciousness, and sculpted ranges of mountains and hills can be seen, providing both orientation and a firm foothold for a new conceptual process that is starting to take place. This is still more potential than actual fact, however, because there is still a heavy curtain of shoulder-length hair obscuring some of the picture for you.

For you, Sandra, geometry was the bridge between inner pictorial experience and outward observation. It had an ordering, clarifying, and thought-strengthening effect, free of any subjective imaginative events. For this reason, it makes sense that you have now been able to take a big step in arithmetic. For the first time in all your years in school, you were the first one to hand in a written math test with all the problems solved correctly!

As usual, your main-lesson books were full of many beautiful things. Whether it's the granite mountains in your mineralogy notebook, freighters on the Rhine, or Manlius riding toward the lictors, your heart and soul are in there, right down to the last little detail. Your compositions are rich in imagery and the action in them is clearly executed. You have an unmistakable talent for creative writing.

In your capable hands, much of what is active in your surroundings is transformed and refined, setting you yourself on the path to inner maturity.

Your class teacher,
Suzanne Kulp

The human soul comes to flower in the world
But is destined to bear fruit in the divine Spirit.

RUDOLF STEINER

As the positive and negative traits of young people of this age reveal, their world has split into likes and dislikes. Extremes are certainly evident, but the new person is also already visible—someone who can function in society and is no longer causing himself or herself or others to suffer.

Sandra came back to school in the fall with a new short hairstyle.

Ten subject reports accompanied this class report.

SEVENTH-GRADE REPORT FOR SANDRA

Dear Sandra,

When you come to school on Monday morning, you always have a lot to giggle and gossip about. Somehow, this always seems to peak during singing time.

When you write an essay, it's almost sure to be one of the best and most interesting in the class.

When it is your turn for clean-up duty, though, the chalk tray is left full of dust.

You complete your main-lesson books neatly; your handwriting is quite legible and there are very few errors in the text. Illustrations, such as those in your history notebook, are drawn with great care.

Whenever you do math, the numbers on the page are always accompanied by sketches of classmates, the teacher, or a little bird.

Sandra, you went through an amazing transformation in seventh grade during our class camping trip. The formerly shy, tender, reserved creature turned into a spokesperson for the class. When the demands of class-work are met, which is easy for you, your interest turns toward the class as a group, looking after it with humor and charm, sometimes as a mediator, sometimes as a taker of initiatives.

When you can keep a picture of the whole class in mind like this, your own strength is available to the whole group in a way that is therapeutic for your classmates and the teacher alike.

Your teacher,
Suzanne Kulp

CLASS TEACHER

A healing social life is found
Only when the whole community
Is mirrored in each human soul
And when the individual soul's own strength
Is active and at home in the community.

RUDOLF STEINER

This last report, a composition in the form of a report on and for her class teacher, will allow us to hear Sandra speak in her own words.

REPORT FOR SUZANNE KULP

Dear Miss Kulp,

It's not so easy to write a report on your teacher—you might even call it just plain hard. So the best thing to do is to dive right in without bothering about fancy sentences. So here you go:

The owl (sorry, I don't mean to compare your looks or disposition to an owl's—after all, this is just a story, so please just skip this part and don't be offended) sat way up in her tree, alternately dozing and watching the lively crowd tumbling around down there at the base of the tree. "How much has changed in the last year!" she sighed. The cute little duckling had turned into a silly goose, the earthworm had turned into a snake ready to strike at the slightest provocation, the tiny little mouse had turned into a big fat fresh-mouthed rat, the rooster had turned into a self-important turkey with no eyes or ears for anything except the hens, and some of those sweet little goldfish had turned into seductive mermaids.

The owl sighed deeply again and tried to get the dust out of her feathers, which were badly rumpled, as she croaked at the class, "This is what I get for dealing with you, gang!" The rat looked up with a big fresh grin on her face.

When dusk began to fall, the owl ordered the whole bunch to follow her. When they got down to the great river, she shooed them all into a boat and untied it. Finally she scratched her head with one long claw and proclaimed hoarsely, "Listen, you guys! It's going to be a long hard trip—one year long, to be precise. I expect you to behave in a somewhat decent and disciplined manner, because it's my job to get you all over to the other side in one piece!" Then she sat down at the tiller. A light wind filled the sails and ruffled the waves. The boat got smaller and smaller and eventually disappeared over the horizon.

Miss Kulp, do you have it figured out yet? Do you know who the owl is and that the river is the Schoolyear River? I wish you nerves of steel and lots of patience for our eighth and final school year together!

Love,
Ratty

Sandra had now developed a conscious relationship with the forces that had been at work shaping her during the early grades by way of the world of images, and this completes the cycle that began, way back when, with a different story.

INDEX